SILENT CRY WITHIN THE CHURCH

OVERCOMING DOMESTIC VIOLENCE IN CHRISTIAN HOMES

CONNIE C. SMITHSON

authorHOUSE

AuthorHouse™
1663 Liberty Drive
Bloomington, IN 47403
www.authorhouse.com
Phone: 833-262-8899

Published by AuthorHouse   03/06/2023

ISBN: 979-8-8230-0218-9 (sc)
ISBN: 979-8-8230-0217-2 (e)

Print information available on the last page.

This book is printed on acid-free paper.

Scripture quotations marked KJV are from the Holy Bible, King James Version (Authorized Version). First published in 1611. Quoted from the KJV Classic Reference Bible, Copyright © 1983 by The Zondervan Corporation.

CONTENTS

DEDICATION

TO THE MEMORY OF my Aunt, Patty Jo-Riddick Pulley, the same evil that plagues many homes, took you from us far too soon. May you rest in peace, until we meet again.

INTRODUCTION

THE FAMILY AS CREATED by God consist of one man and one woman. In God's plan for the family, man and woman were to come together as husband and wife for the sole purpose of helping one another and populating the Earth. It is Gods will that Christ be at the center of every marriage, and that the husband love his wife just as Christ loves the church and that the wife submit to her husband, as unto the Lord (Ephesians 5:22&24). The Bible teaches that the husband is the head of the wife, even as Christ is head of the church. These scriptures taken out of context have caused many Pastors and church leaders to counsel women suffering abuse at the hand of their husbands, to stay in a relationship that has cost her–her very life. This book inspired by God, is designed to explain the family unit, the way God intended for it to be. In addition, Domestic Violence will be discussed and evaluated in great length, including statistics; laws; the cycle of abuse; children witnessing abuse; testimonies from survivors; my own family's testimony of how silence kills; Jesus as the answer; and resources. Oftentimes, Domestic Violence is seen by Law Enforcement, the Department of Social Service's and Domestic Violence Advocacy agencies with help made available, but too often it goes unnoticed in the church. It is my hope that this book will raise awareness within the church community and help leaders to better understand how to resolve the issue of Domestic Violence behind the stain glass windows, and as a result see men and women set free from the effects and causes of abuse.

CHAPTER ONE

MARRIAGE, FAMILY, AND THE CHURCH

A DAM AND EVE WERE the first man and woman created by God, after creating them, marriage was instituted, as God made them husband and wife. The husband-wife relationship ordained by God is the foundation for the family. The husband and wife become the father and mother of children, and this makes up the family unit, as God said it should be. Jesus in Matthew 19, affirmed Gods institution for marriage, when He said in verse 4, *"Have you not read, that He which made them at the beginning made them male and female."* God gave Eve to be Adam's wife, and she became his equal. This is how marriage was intended by God, for the husband and wife to be equal and to carry out different roles in their daily living. The equality between a husband and wife are emphasized in the New Testament. The book of I Corinthians Chapter 11 plainly states in verses 8, 11, and 12 *"For the man is not of the woman; but the woman of the man."* V.11 *"Nevertheless neither is the man without the woman, neither the woman without the man, in the Lord."* V.12 *"For as the woman is of the man, even so is the man also by woman, but all things of God."* In the book of Ephesians Chapter 5 husbands and wives both are given instructions for how they are to treat one another. Wives are to submit to their husbands, as unto the Lord. This means that first and foremost, the wife is to submit to Christ as Lord and Master, not the husband. Verse 23 reads, *"that the husband is the head of the wife, even as Christ is the Head of the Church, and He is Savior of the body."* This simply put is saying, if the husband is following the Lord in a proper way, the obedience she shows her husband is to be regarded as obedience provided to Christ. Likewise, Husbands are to love their wives even as Christ also loved the church and gave Himself for it. In other words, the answer to marital problems, is for the husband and wife to make Christ the center of their marriage, always putting Christ first. God designed marriage to be a covenant relationship through which the husband and wife experience love, respect, companionship, and physical relationship.

The husband, wife, and children are only one type of family unit. In addition, there is another type of family that believers in Christ Jesus, become a part of, and it is the church family. Believers are members of God's household, or God's family. The term "church family" best describes the relationship that people share when they attend the same church. Believers not only attend the same church, listen to sermons and worship God together, they go through life together, just as with their biological family. It has even been said that believers are closer to their church family than some of their own blood relatives, because believers are considered brothers and sisters in Christ, and immediate, as well as, extended family members who are not believers, have little in common with them other than their blood line.

Members of the church family are often there to provide support during the hardships of life. They also come together for events such as, marriage, the arrival of a new baby, baby dedication services, and baptism. Another aspect of the believer's involvement with their church family is found when they disciple one another, engage in Bible Studies and share the love of God, growing deeper in their relationship with God. As wonderful as being a part of a church family seems to be, there are times when believers are hurt, or disappointed by a fellow believer.

The enemy works overtime to try and bring division to the church. Although, believers are taught, and the word clearly states that believers are to show love and forgiveness, they are still human, living in a body of flesh, and while the sin nature does not or should not have control, believers are still capable of slipping and saying or doing the wrong things at times. Seeking God's word for wisdom on how to navigate those difficulties is always best practice for the believer. When the church family finds they are struggling, it is best to talk through it, pray, and ask God for His help. There is also another, important element of the church family, and that is the Pastor.

The Pastor is considered the Shepherd of the flock, the glue that holds it all together. As a Pastor, the expectations, are high. First, the Pastor must exercise a saving faith in

Christ Jesus as Lord and Savior. Second, he or she is responsible for living their life in relationship to the Lord. They are to be faithful stewards of Christ, thereby living a biblically balanced life. This will in return help them to serve others in a most effective way. Pastors have many duties to carry out. Their responsibilities go far beyond preparing a message for Sunday morning and midweek Bible study. When someone is hospitalized, they are a first responder, when someone gets married, they have a wedding to perform, when death comes knocking, the Pastor is either there or getting the call to come at once. When there are marital problems, the Pastor is expected to be available, when someone is depressed and contemplating suicide, they reach out to the Pastor. The Pastors phone never stops ringing—it is often like a 24-hour hotline.

Out of all the circumstances mentioned, one of the greatest tragedies the Pastor deals with is Domestic Violence, among individuals that make up the church family. Primarily because he or she has the obligation of counseling both, the victim, and the batterer, who most likely are going to leave and go home together. If there are children involved, the Pastor has the responsibility of calling Child Protective Services, if the violence occurred in front of the children. While Domestic Violence in the church puts the Pastor in a position of having to make some strenuous decisions, the greater impact of Domestic Violence in the church is felt by the man or woman sitting on the pew, teaching Sunday school, serving on a board, singing in the choir, working the nursery or perhaps leaving with the Pastor to go home, with the same bruises they came to church with, as well as, the risk of threats, degrading remarks, and belittling comments that were screamed at them the night before. The ones who cry alone at home embarrassed to tell anyone, especially their church family—the silent ones.

The silent ones are not always the poor living in low income housing, but rather belong to the middle class, who appear to be a highly functional Christian family and are strong financial supporters of the church. Domestic Violence among partners is more prominent in the church than Pastors would like to admit and unfortunately, it gets brushed under the rug, so to speak. At times, men and women who suffer abuse have a Pastor who is quick to use Ephesians five out of context, or they are told divorce is not an option and that God would not be pleased with them leaving. While God does not condone divorce, He also does not expect His sons and daughters to be used as a punching bag, verbally or otherwise by their spouse.

Women especially, who are given this misinformation, many times stay, until it is too late and the one who promised to love her until death becomes the reason—she is dead. There are protocols the leaders can implement to try and deter Domestic Violence from occurring among couples in the church. Pastors can confront the issue by informing members that Domestic Violence is a sin. It is rare that a message is preached on Domestic Violence as a sin from behind the pulpit. In addition, they can do things like recognizing October as Domestic Violence awareness month, invite experts to talk to the congregation throughout the year, put on seminars, provide online resources, partner with other agencies and make it an integral part of premarital counseling. Many Pastors have never been trained to understand how to configure their pastoral care to respond effectively, and Pastors are not always aware of the violence in the home, due to both parties hiding it so well.

Once the victim feels ready to disclose the violence being perpetrated against them, they generally reach out to the Pastor first. However, if they do not feel comfortable telling the Pastor, their first choice could possibly be a church family member, perhaps someone, such as, a prayer partner. No man or woman should be put in a position of feeling like they have no one to turn to for help, especially among their church family. Church leaders need to execute practices to help make the church a safe place for men and women suffering at the hands of their spouse. As a Christian that is a part of a church, pay attention to those around you, if something seems off, ask questions, you never know when the victim has reached a breaking point and is waiting for that right moment to finally share their deepest secrets and no longer cry in silence, but out loud for all to hear.

When the person is ready to talk about the violence they have endured, it is important to listen, and show them respect and empathy, do not doubt or question what they are saying. If they feel their life is in immediate danger, go to the Pastor who is a mandated reporter and he or she should make the victim aware of their obligation to call the proper authorities. Have a list of referrals available and always be conscious that intervention increases risk to the victim, as well as, any children who may be involved. The Pastor should stress to the person that God abhors abuse and encourage them to take action to separate from the abusive spouse.

Gods design for marriage is broken by abuse and scripture does not mandate that any man or woman should stay in a marriage that is placing their life in danger or breaking down their mental state. Whether it is the husband or wife being abused, Christian or not, no human being should have to live a life of fear, feeling trapped in a relationship that could ultimately take their life. Domestic Violence is a versatile experience that men and women in the church suffer.

The impact of the violence on victims often persists for years after the abusive relationship has ended. It is vital that church leaders, along with the congregation work together to be a support to victims of Domestic Violence, thereby, silencing the violence and allowing the cries to be heard. Domestic Violence in the church is a reality that must not be ignored or overlooked, lives are at stake and for every life that is lost, because leaders simply chose not to deal with it, that victim's blood is on their hands.

CHAPTER TWO

UNDERSTANDING DOMESTIC VIOLENCE

P ROVIDING RESOURCES AND MAKING not only the church community, but the community, as a whole; aware of Domestic Violence and all that it entails is critical. Many people in leadership such as Pastors are not acquainted with the laws or the facts surrounding Domestic Violence. As hard as it is to believe, there are some people living in a Domestic Violence environment, who are oblivious to their relationship being abusive, simply because they are not being Physically abused. Throughout this next Chapter, I hope to bring insight to every aspect of Domestic Violence as well as the victims right to a protective order and what to expect in obtaining one. It is my hope to help people gain a greater perspective of what Domestic Violence really is. It is important to note that 1 in 4 women and 1 in 9 men experience intimate partner, physical, emotional, and sexual abuse. Having already acknowledged that men do suffer at the hands of women and experience Domestic Violence, because it is primarily women who fall victim to this injustice, the remainder of the book will be geared toward women.

Feminists defined the battering of women in the early 1970's not as the *problem* but as the *symptom* of a much larger and more pervasive problem: a patriarchal society in which men hold disproportionate power over valued resources and in which women are subservient to men both within marriage and in all important facets of society. To one degree or another, violence against women is socially sanctioned. Steve Marks (Men's Program of Marin) had this to say about the conditions of women: "The person and labor of women is deemed and denigrated; for police officers it is often lethal to interfere in man's expression of marital and cultural rights." As with men elsewhere, men in the United States hint that the stress of their economic status is justification enough for their choices of violence. Yet women, who are statistically twice as stressed, rarely attack their partners. Language currently used in discussing violence against women does not accurately reflect *who* is being victimized and to what extent. "Domestic Violence," "spouse abuse," and "family violence" are all euphemisms for the statistically more likely occurrence of violence against women—*not* men. Other words such as "dispute," "spat," or "quarrel" prevent the public from understanding the true nature of battering because they trivialize the actual level of violence against women.

The three words "abuse," "violence," and "battery" are used interchangeably. These three words involve both the concept of *intention* to intimidate, coerce, or establish dominance, as well as the violent act itself. They refer not only to physical abuse but also to emotional, sexual, and financial abuse. We think most often of physical abuse, but it is important to remember that emotional abuse can be as damaging to a woman's emotional well-being as physical abuse is to her physical well-being. Examples include, but are not limited to, enforced isolation of the woman from her friends, family, church, or workplace; constant threats that her children will be taken away; and destruction of the woman's self-esteem due to inconsistent expectations on the part of the abuser. Another form of assault clearly described by battered women is marital rape.

Specific actions of emotional and financial abuse include the following:

1. Insulting her friends and making it hard for her to spend time with them
2. Monitoring phone calls, listening, commenting on each call, limiting her privacy
3. Making her dependent on him for transportation
4. Keeping her economically dependent
5. Not allowing her personal growth: enrolling in school, doing artwork, writing, developing other skills, etc.
6. Making it hard for her to go to school, church, work, women's groups, bowling, softball, etc.
7. Strictly defining roles and limiting her to housework and children ("keeping the wife barefoot and pregnant").

Domestic Violence Resources for Enhanced Practice Accessed September 7, 2004

Behaviors displayed by the abuser can be violent or nonviolent. Using intimidation, making him or her afraid by using looks, actions, or gestures; smashing things; destroying property; abusing pets; and displaying weapons.

- **Non-intimidating behaviors:** talking and acting so that he or she feels safe and comfortable expressing himself or herself and doing things.
- **Using emotional abuse:** putting him or her down, making him or her feel bad about himself or herself, calling names, making him or her think he's/she's crazy, playing mind games, humiliating him or her, making him or her feel guilty.
- **Respect:** listening to him or her nonjudgmentally, being emotionally affirming and understanding, valuing opinions.
- **Using isolation:** controlling what he or she does, who he or she sees and talks to, what he or she reads, and where he or she goes; limiting his or her outside involvement; using jealousy to justify actions.
- **Trust and support:** supporting goals in life and respecting his or her right to his or her feelings, friend, activities, and opinions.
- **Minimizing, denying, and blaming:** making light of the abuse and not taking his or her concerns about it seriously, saying the abuse didn't happen,

shifting responsibility for abusive behavior, saying he or she caused it.

- **Honesty and accountability:** accepting responsibility for self, acknowledging past use of violence, admitting being wrong, communicating openly and truthfully.

- **Using children:** making him or her feel guilty about the children, using the children to relay messages, using visitation to harass him or her, threatening to take children away.

- **Responsible parenting:** sharing parental responsibilities, being a positive nonviolent role model for the children.

- **Using male privilege:** treating him or her like a servant, making all the big decisions, acting like the "master of the castle," being the to define men's and women's roles.

- **Shared responsibility:** mutually agreeing on a fair distribution of work, making family decision together.

- **Using economic abuse:** preventing he or she from getting or keeping a job, making him or her ask for money, giving him or her an allowance, taking his or her money, not letting him or her know about or have access to family income.

- **Using coercion and threats:** making and/or carrying out threats to hurt him or her; threatening to leave him or her, to commit suicide, or to report him or her to welfare; making him or her drop charges; making him or her do illegal things.

- **Negotiation and fairness:** seeking mutually satisfying resolutions to conflict, accepting change, and being willing to compromise.

Each U.S. State should have policies and practice recommendations and an implementation plan that maximizes the safety of all family members, empowers victims, and holds perpetrators of Domestic Violence (DV) and child maltreatment accountable. State task forces should include a multidisciplinary representation ranging from child advocates, advocates against Domestic Violence, courts, law enforcement, and public health officials to public instruction, human services representatives, victims, judges, legislators, researchers, and citizens. Such task force should further develop policy and protocol around the following areas:

- Funding
- Courts and law enforcement
- Community-based services
- Child Protective Services (CPS)

Intimate partner violence is primarily a crime against women. In 2001, women accounted for 85% of the victims of intimate partner violence, and men accounted for approximately 15% of the victims. In 1998 it was reported that 3 million women are physically abused by their husbands or boyfriends per year, in 2021 the statistics showed and increase to 19 million women annually are abused by an intimate partner. Women of all races are about equally vulnerable to violence by an intimate partner.

The following additional information is from Lenore E. Walker in *The Battered Woman* (pp. 16-25):

At least one third of all families have experienced physical violence. Half of all families report some kind of Domestic Violence. About one third of the batterers beat their children. Interestingly, most men who batter their wives are not violent in other aspects of their lives. In fact, they share with psychopathic personalities the trait of using their extraordinary charm as a manipulative technique. Batterers can be playful, attentive, sensitive, exciting, and affectionate to their partners, especially during the "honeymoon stages" that tend to occur between bouts of battering. It is estimated that a small percentage, about 0.01%, of batterers can learn more appropriate ways to handle their emotions. Unfortunately, few longstanding battering relationships can change for the better. **If a man has battered before the wedding, he will continue afterward; a marriage license seems to be a license to batter. Violence often escalates over the years to homicidal and suicidal proportions.**

The myth that battered women are masochistic has been used by social agencies and batterers to vindicate physical abuse of women. Likewise, saying that battered women are crazy, attempts to blame the woman's negative personality and the characteristics for her having been battered. Sometimes, when a woman's survival strategies seem unusual to medical professionals (predominantly men), the woman is labeled crazy or depressed. Few women call the police because experience has taught them that the police are seldom sympathetic and often ineffective. Studies show that women who have sought beneficial intervention rarely remarry a violent man. An equally inaccurate myth is that children need their father even if he is violent—or, put another way, that battered women should stay "for the sake of the children." Although children generally love their violent fathers, most say they prefer living with just one parent to living with the violence and fear so common in such homes. *Even more important, though, is the problem that children who stay in violent homes often learn how to batter or to accept battering, and so repeat in adulthood the same violent patterns of their parents.*

"Why Does Someone Abuse?"

Many people think, "If it's that bad someone would just leave," or "Someone must be getting something out of it since he or she is staying." Instead of asking why someone stays, the question to ask is, "Why does someone abuse?" This requires a shift in thinking, and accountability by perpetrators. Social work professionals should lead the way in the move away from a victim-blaming attitude toward a systematic approach that holds perpetrators accountable for their violent actions and behaviors. This can be accomplished through engaging the family using family-centered principles of practice and involvement with the family. It will manifest itself in the way families are spoken to and approached by social workers.

It is never the adult victim's fault that he or she is being abused. The adult victim may experience low self-esteem or be physically, emotionally, and/or financially dependent on his or her abuser as a result of the domestic violence, but these factors do not cause or create his or her victimization. Rather than being abused because they have poor self-esteem, adult victims may experience poor self-esteem resulting in them being targets of systematic, deliberate, and constant emotional and psychological abuse aimed at stripping them of their sense of self-worth. Additionally, abusers are strategic in isolating their victims, ensuring that their emotional and psychological abuse will go unnoticed and unchallenged by people who care about and support their partners.

Statements a Domestic Violence Victim will make:

- I could never find another man to love the way I love him.
- Without him, I have nothing to live for.
- I know exactly what it about him I love.
- No one could ever understand him the way I do.
- I suppose I should be interested in other people and activities, but I just want to be with him.
- We help each other to explore new possibilities in life.
- The idea of making love to another man is unthinkable.
- Whenever I am a few minutes late or want to be alone, he thinks I'm with another man.

- Loving him makes me feel more loving toward other people.
- I try to keep on my "rose-colored glasses" and see only the best in him.
- I love him and I cannot stand the thought of his being with anyone else.
- I hope he never leaves me, but if it come to that I will be okay.
- He would never love another woman the way he loves me.
- Often, I feel better when I am away from him, yet I find myself calling him against my better judgement.
- I feel that I am nothing without him.
- I never let him see me without makeup or with curlers in my hair, I want him always to see me at my best.
- He brings out the best in me.
- I do not know why I love him, I just do.
- When things are going well with us, I do not need anyone but him.
- He has many of the qualities I value and that I am trying to develop in myself.
- He is so much smarter and more capable than I am, he seems know everything about everything.
- When I try to imagine never seeing him again, I feel empty. It is wonderful to spend time with him at sports, work, or having fun together with other people, and I enjoy being by myself or with women friends, too.

- He is special; I do not know why he is interested in an ordinary person like me.
- Without me, he has nothing to live for.
- He wants me to feel good whether I am with him or not.
- This time he means it. He is really going to change.
- I know he loves me because he wants to know where I am every minute.
- I like to hear about the good times he had when he has been with other people.

Cycle of Violence

Starts out as an argument followed by slapping or shoving may lead, eventually, to kicking, punching, choking, or use of a weapon. The woman may begin to anticipate the violence. This increases her fear, depression, and anger, and/or decreases her confidence in her rights in the relationship.

There are three stages in a recurring cycle of battering:

1. Tension building
2. Explosion
3. Love

In the first phase of the cycle, the tension first starts to build and then to increase. The woman may try to prevent the violence from increasing but the tension continues to build until a certain point is reached. This results in the second state—a single, acute battering episode when the violence erupts. The third phase or "honeymoon phase," follows.

This stage may bring reduced tension. The man may act remorseful, kind and loving, and the woman, wanting to believe that he will change, accepts this reconciliation as reinforcement to stay in the relationship. Some women do not consider this a honeymoon stage but merely a respite from the acute battering and tension. Additionally, leaving an abusive relationship can also be dangerous for victims. Research suggests that the initial length of time after a victim has left his or her abuser is an especially dangerous time, and that as many as 75% of DV victims who are killed are murdered during the separation. If the abuser has all the economic and social status, leaving can cause additional problems for the victim. Leaving can mean living in fear, losing child custody, losing financial support, and experiencing harassment at work. Adult victims experience shame, embarrassment, and isolation. An adult victim may not leave immediately because:

- He or she realistically fears that the violence will escalate, possibly even become fatal if he or she attempts to leave.
- Friends and family may not support his or her leaving.
- He or she knows the difficulties of single parenting in reduced financial circumstances.
- There is a mixture of good times, love, and hope along with intimidation, fear, and manipulation.
- He or she may not know about or have access to safety and support.

The reality is that most adult victims do not stay in abusive relationships without attempting to leave. As with many significant life changes, leaving is a process. On average, victims leave and return five to seven times before they make a final break with their abusive partner. In the past, Child Protective Service workers have required that adult victims leave, to ensure the children's safety. While leaving may be a viable option for some victims, other victims may decide to stay. If the victim chooses to leave, it is a potentially violent time, and these cases must be handled carefully. Leaving a Domestic Violence relationship requires thoughtful, detailed safety planning in which the adult victim identifies what he or she needs to keep him or her safe. It is also important to recognize that while leaving and returning is a part of the overall process of escaping Domestic Violence, this can produce negative consequences for the child. The instability that results can negatively impact the child. It is important to look for any changes in the child's functioning at home, school, and church. Perpetrators of Domestic Violence may cause harm to children not only by exposing them to abuse and violence but also by displacing them and creating the need for constant transition.

Hart, B. National Coalition Against
Domestic Violence, 1988

Victims of Domestic Violence may

- Experience depression
- Feel emotionally distressed
- Demonstrate dependency on the relationship

- Feel afraid, helpless, ashamed, defensive, guilty, isolated
- Deny or minimize the assaults
- Defend their partners
- Have a history of family violence

There is a complex interplay of internal and external constraints that often imprisons a woman in a violent home or a battering situation. Fear brought on by a combination of continued threats and violence, and absence of provisions for safety are universally identified as deterrents to any action. Other studies indicate that battered women often do not believe that they can escape from the batterer's denomination or control. Many women have left only to be followed and persecuted or killed by their abusers. Factors influencing why a woman would decide to stay in an abusive relationship or how long she decides to stay are as follows:

- The severity and frequency of the violence
- The woman's personal resources and skills
- Her economic situation
- Children
- Her religious beliefs and support system
- A history of abuse in her family of origin
- The responsiveness and accessibility of external resources: Police, Court System, Social Services and Church

North Carolina Division of Social Services, Domestic Violence Policy Training Participant Manual January 2005

To let go

- Does not mean to stop caring; it means knowing I cannot do it for someone else.
- Is not to enable but to allow learning from natural consequences
- Is to admit powerlessness, which means understanding that the outcome is not in my hands.
- Is not to try to change or blame another; it is to make the most of myself.
- Is not to care for but to care about.

Getting a Domestic Violence Protective Order Without Hiring an Attorney

This information was prepared as a public service by attorneys in North Carolina, based on a written law as of January 1, 1990. It is not intended to be a complete statement of the law or to apply in every situation. Because laws may change from time to time you should see an attorney if you have questions about any of the following information. Because 95% of battered persons are women, this information assumes that a woman is using it. However, the law provides protection from Domestic Violence for both men and women.

Abuse is slapping, hitting, grabbing, pushing, choking, kicking, wrestling, hair pulling, punching, or any other act that causes injury. Abuse can also be threatening to do any of these things and putting you in danger of serious injury. This law applies to you husband, your ex-husband, or your live-in boyfriend. A Domestic Violence Protective Order is also called a restraining order, temporary restraining order (TRO), or a 50B order. It is a paper that is signed by a judge and says that your husband, ex-husband, or boyfriend should not abuse you or your children. The DV protective order can do more than just protect you and your children. It can also:

- Order him not to assault, threaten, abuse, follow, harass, or interfere with you and your children either in person or on the telephone.
- Allow you to live in the home that you two shared and order him to move and not return.
- Give you possession of personal property such as clothing, toiletries, and tools of trade.
- Give you possession and use of the car.
- Order him to stay away from your home, your workplace, your school, the children's school and daycare, or any place where you are seeking shelter.
- Give you temporary custody of the minor children and order him to pay child support.
- Tell the police or Sheriff's Department to remove him from the home and help you return to the home.

If you or your children are in danger, ask for an Ex Parte Order in your complaint and motion. Usually, in any court action, the judge will listen to both sides before making a decision. However, in domestic violence cases the law allows the judge (magistrate) to sign an *Ex Parte* Protective Order.

This order is signed before your husband or boyfriend is notified that you have filed a complaint and before he tells the judge his side of the story. (*Ex Parte* means from one side only.) An *Ex Parte* order will last for no more than ten days. Within the ten days there will be a hearing to decide if you can get protection for a longer time. At that hearing the defendant will get a chance to tell his side of the story. If you want an *Ex Parte* order, be sure to check Box two at the bottom of page one of the Complaint and Motion form. The forms to get the ball rolling can be obtained by going to the Clerk of Court at the courthouse. Fill out the form carefully. You will be the Plaintiff (the person making the complaint), and your husband or boyfriend will be the defendant (the person accused of abuse). Write your husband's name or boyfriend's full name and home and work addresses in the box called "Name and Address of Defendant." Give a phone number, if possible. After you fill out the form, sign it in front of a notary public or court clerk. Second, you will fill out the top part of the Civil Summons. Write your name and safe mailing address and phone number where you can be reached. (If you are staying at a shelter or other secret place, do not write the actual street address.) Write the defendant's name, home and work addresses, and phone number, if possible. Write directions on the summons if the defendants address is hard to find. Third, file the complaint with the Court Clerk and pay the filing and service fees. Fill out the Complaint and Motion form and file it with Court Clerk. Pay the clerk a filing fee, plus a fee for the Sheriff to serve the papers (deliver them to the defendant). If you cannot afford these fees, you may be able to file without pay. Ask the clerk for a form called Petition to Sue as Pauper (A pauper is a poor reason.) You will have to sign this form in front of a notary public or the clerk. Fourth, Ask the Clerk for the date and time of your hearing. If you asked for an *Ex Parte* order in your Complaint and Motion form, let the clerk know this. The clerk must set a date and time for you to meet with the judge. You should be given a chance to appear before a judge within two or three days for you *Ex Parte* hearing. Whether or not you asked for an *Ex Parte,* you will have a hearing for a Domestic Violence Protective Order. This hearing should be held within a week to ten days. Last, before the hearing for a Domestic Violence Protective Order, a copy of the court papers must be served (delivered) to the defendant by the Sheriff or police. If you received an *Ex Parte* order, it will be served with the other papers.

After court if you and your partner made the decision to stay together, form a network with friends or family so you have a place to stay for a few days if you need to. Make clear the expectations of all persons involved: how long you can stay, whether you will be able or expected to help with groceries, etc. Pack a few clothes for you and your children and leave them with the friend you might be staying with. Rehearse going to your temporary safe place from your home so that the route will become familiar to you. Rehearse your departure, especially if you leave while he is home. Use plausible, mundane excuses: "I need some milk for the kids, I'll take them with me, so they won't bother you." In other words, think about being in a situation where your partner's behavior is about to get out of control and come up with different strategies that could help you get out of the house and to your safe place before he hurts you or the children. Once outside the door, just keep going. Remember, you are the expert about your situation. Use the strategies that will work best for you. Make copies of important documents, including birth certificates, legal documents, medical and school records, and keepsake photographs. Put the originals in a safe-deposit box. Use a friend's address for the bank so that your mail cannot be intercepted. (This will also be advisable if you establish a secret account in case you need to leave permanently.) Try and have a safe place nearby that the children can walk to, if they get out, but you cannot.

With the multiple resources, outlets, warnings, and descriptions outlined throughout this Chapter concerning Domestic Violence and helping victims, I have been remiss in acknowledging there is also help available for batterers, although the only real help is found in a relationship with Christ Jesus. There are real barriers to leaving a violent relationship, and there are no simple, easy solutions. In addition, given the resources available, resources are still lacking. The church should not be one of those resources. What victims and families endure is unimaginable for most of us, and is prominent in our communities, including within our churches. Its important to know the signs to look for and the proper action to take when abuse is suspected among the church family. The action the Pastor takes today, could prevent him from having to preach a funeral tomorrow.

CHAPTER THREE

TESTIMONIES OF ABUSE

T HE FOLLOWING TESTIMONIES ARE real accounts from women who were involved in Domestic Violence relationships. Their names have been fictionalized for their protection. A few of them give an account of what they experienced behind the walls of their church once the violence in their home was exposed. Evidence that there needs to be more done in the church to bring awareness, prevention, and protection.

Janes story:

Jane had been married to her husband for ten years. She became pregnant with her first child shortly after she and her husband were married. Currently they have three children, ages nine, seven and six. Even, from the beginning her husband made all the decisions for their family.

The first time he hit her was when she was pregnant with her first child. They had come home from her mother's house and he was angry that he had forgotten to buy a particular food item that he likes, he slapped her. She thought it was just an isolated event and did not anticipate him doing it again.

Since then, he has hit, kicked, choked, slapped, and burned her. The physical abuse does not happen that often, maybe once a month. Mainly, when she does something he does not like, such as visiting her mother or talking on the phone to a friend. He also calls her degrading names such as prostitute and whore. He tells her that he will take the children and go to his mother's home if she is not a good wife. He refuses to let her get a job, even though the children are in school. Jane's background would qualify her for many different employment opportunities. The only money he allows her is enough to buy a few groceries.

He is jealous and possessive. A few months ago, he became angry because she was late getting home from the store. He accused her of seeing another man and punched a hole in the door between the kitchen and the living room. Her sons were there and saw this, he yelled at them to go to their rooms. Jane also overheard him asking their seven-year-old son if he had ever heard her talking to other men. He then told their son that Jane was crazy and to watch her and let him know if she does anything strange.

A few months ago, Jane's husband came home late with his friends and made her cook them food. He started joking with his friends about how much she weighed, saying she is like all other women who let themselves go once they get married. After his friends left, he woke Jane up and forced her to have sex with him, even though she did not want to and was feeling sick. He told Jane she knew what would happen if she did not obey him. Recently, Jane tried to talk to her husband about the abuse. He got angry. He said he does not hurt her anymore than what is expected from a husband, and that he thinks, he is too nice to her. He went on to tell Jane, that if he was too harsh at times it was her fault for not being a good wife and letting herself become unattractive. Jane said, she loves her husband, but does not think she can continue to live with him. Her husband has threatened to kill her, the children and himself if she leaves. She has no job or money and would not be able to find a place to go.

Mary's story:

Mary and her husband attended church on a regular basis and had been faithful members for years. Her husband was well known in the community, Deacon in the church, and she filled in where needed. One Sunday they had a fight before church and during a couple's class, the teacher noticed that the body language between them seemed to suggest that maybe they were having some difficulties. The teacher also noticed that they seemed to be noticeably aggravated with one another. Mary's husband began to not come to class, and would show up just in time for service, which raised a red flag. In addition, the teacher noticed that Mary was using excessive makeup to try and cover a large bruise on her face and a black eye.

He made a lady in the church aware and in the most appropriate way they confronted Mary and ask her what happened. During the initial conversation, Mary was reluctant to discuss any personal problems and said she was hit by a foul ball at her son's baseball game. A week later she had more bruises and became emotional when she was questioned again. During the conversation she began to disclose how unhappy she was and how her husband was stressed and struggling with some things. She repeated several times, "he's a good man." "He's just stressed out."

After a couple of Sundays passed, Mary was outside of the church crying and one of the ladies went to check on her. She told them she was done and could not take it anymore. The Pastor was made aware of Mary's situation and at first said "let Mary and her husband work it out." When confronted again, the Pastor said, "I will take care of it." There was no investigation. The Pastor never checked into it. The husband denied any wrong. Mary filed for divorce and moved out of the house, taking the children with her. The husband stepped down as Deacon in the church. Today, Mary is doing great and her children are thriving.

Annas story:

Anna was married to a Pastor and shared in the duties of their local church. On the surface, at church, they, along with their children, appeared to be a close family. Middle class working family that had it all together. One day their son revealed to a friend who also attended their church that his parents were fighting a lot. It began to become apparent within the church that something was wrong between the couple, and so they were approach by a friend in the church who ask them if everything was okay at home. The Pastor and his wife not wanting their personal life made public, simply played it off, and said everything was fine, their children misunderstood and were exaggerating. Later, the Pastor confided in another friend that he and his wife had been having some real fights and the confrontations were emotional, as well as physical.

For a while Anna and her husband put on a front at church, and so to their church family, things seem to have improved, but they had become far worse. One night an altercation between them led to the Police being called to their home, they both faced several charges. It was later learned by their church family and people in the community, that both Anna and her husband were struggling with alcohol, as well as pornography.

The couple went through a series of counseling sessions that revealed deeper issues, resulting in the church becoming divided. Some of the congregation wanted them to resign immediately and others wanted them to get help, work it out and stay. Ultimately, Anna and her husband divorced and left the church.

Sarah's story:

Sarah attended a Christian college where the males lived on one side of the campus and females on the opposite side. Sarah met a boy there and they began dating. Her boyfriend was the son of a well-known Pastor/leader in a certain denomination, his family were also financial supporters of the school. Sarah and her boyfriend had not been dating long, when one day he invited her over to his dorm. Sarah, knowing girls were not allowed in the male dorms, went anyway. Her boyfriend reassured her it would be okay and that no one would find out. Sarah thought it would be harmless, he said they were going to hang out and watch movies.

While Sarah was there, her boyfriend began to force himself on her. She tried to push him away but was not successful in doing so. He raped her. As she ran out of his dorm screaming, another student heard her and looked in the direction of the scream. He saw Sarah running, screaming for help, and her boyfriend laughing.

Although the school's policy stated such conduct would result in expulsion, her boyfriend was permitted to stay in school. Sarah also stayed in school and was coerced to retract her accusations of rape. A couple of years later after they both had graduated, Sarah married someone different and is happy in her relationship with her husband. The young man, accused of rape, had also married but in his case, he had not changed. He assaulted his wife, was arrested for a domestic dispute which led to violence and convicted of assault.

Karen's story:

Karen and her husband have been married for thirty years. During their thirty-year marriage they have gone to the same church and even served as missionaries. What her church family did not know is that behind closed doors at home and on the mission field, Karen was being physically, emotionally, and Spiritually abused by her husband that everyone adored. Karen's husband manipulated everyone he met, convincing them, he was a great man of God and wonderful husband to his wife, as well as father to his children.

Karen felt as though she had no options for help because domestic abuse would mean she and her husband being removed from the mission field. Karen loved the people she served on the mission field and knew God had called her to be a missionary. As Karen's children became older, the abuse continued to worsen, until Karen reached a breaking point, no longer able to endure the abuse, she reached out to her Pastor and disclosed to him how she had been living. Her Pastor, although in disbelief, encouraged Karen to leave her husband and to explore other avenues in missions. Karen divorced her husband and today lives alone, dealing with the damaging effects of Post Traumatic Stress Disorder (PTSD), false guilt, and health issues caused by years of trauma.

Karen was blessed to have a Pastor who understood Domestic Violence, as well as the true word of God as it pertains to marriage and divorce. Her Pastor encouraging her to leave, most likely saved her life. When the church affirms an abusive man's role as the head of the home, it gives carte blanche to men who need to be in control. It sanctions abusive behaviors and leaves the wife with no options.

Natasha's story:

When Natasha first met her husband, he was outgoing, funny, and they immediately hit it off. During their courtship, he always put her first and treated her with kindness. She fell for him quickly and it was not long before he was proposing marriage. After they were married within a couple of months Natasha's, now husband, became jealous, doing things such as checking her phone, and emails. He would not allow her to have any male friends despite him having female friends.

Natasha's husband went from being jealous, to calling her names, and throwing things at her. He would break things in the home, and punch holes in the walls. When he did not get his way or had a bad day at work he would come home and take it out on her by kicking her, slapping, and punching her. Natasha, went to her Pastor and disclosed the abuse to him, but she was told to stay in her marriage. Her Pastor told her that God does not like divorce and that maybe she and her husband could try Christian counseling. One night Natasha's husband came home and beat her to the point of being unconscious, when she came to, she was able to call for help, the police came and arrested her husband, she was taken to the hospital for her injuries and once discharged she connected with a Domestic Violence agency that was able to help her out of the home. Natasha filed for divorce and today is doing well.

Brenda's story:

Brenda is thirty-five years old, the mother of three children and had married the love of her life. In the beginning Brenda's marriage seemed to be a perfect love story, but it was not long before that quickly changed, and it became an abusive one. Brenda's husband began to have repeated affairs which led Brenda to confront him. As a result, Brenda's husband beat her. In addition, to beating her, her husband called her names, abused her emotionally, and made her think that she deserved the violence.

Brenda's husband, like many, was well known in the community, a pillar in their church, everyone thought of him as a great guy, who would never do anything to harm anyone. When Brenda had finally endured the abuse for years, she reached a breaking point, and confided in one of the ladies at her church. She was told to try and talk to her husband and work things out, that walking away from the marriage was not what she needed to do.

Brenda stayed with her husband, until she was faced with the realization one day of her children acting out, as a result, of witnessing the abuse. One day while her husband was at work, Brenda told a friend what she had been going through at home, and her friend helped her to get out. Brenda filed for a divorce and today is married to a man who loves her and her children, as his own.

The stories of these women are only a few stories of those who have suffered abuse at the hands of their husbands. Domestic Violence is happening among middle class church couples who are both professing Christianity, with conservative upbringing, as well as couples without those advantages. Twenty-eight percent of reformed church members experience abuse in their marriage. It is true that most churches do not tolerate violence in the family and that there are Pastors such as Karen's who know the proper action to take, as well as how to counsel in an effective way, according to the word of God. Some Pastors will take the victim by the hand and guide them through the process needed, to move past the effects of Domestic Violence. Although, the trauma can have an emotional impact, that last a lifetime, God can bring peace and comfort to the victim, helping them to move forward in life and not let past violence continue to control them.

CHAPTER FOUR

SILENCE KILLS—
MY FAMILY'S STORY

PATTY JO RIDDICK-PULLEY WAS born July 1st 1961. Raised in Rural Gates County, North Carolina, she along with her older siblings were a part of a loving traditional family. Her father was a hard worker, always busy farming, and her mother was a homemaker who occupied her time with working the garden, tending flowers, and running the local grocery store she and her husband owned and operated together.

Patty Jo grew up surrounded by family who not only loved her but protected her as well. Once she was old enough to start school, she proved to be an exceptional student always earning "A's," in addition to academics, she was involved in all sports, many different clubs and other extracurricular activities, including dance and the North Carolina beauty pageant. Everyone that came to know her, loved her. Holidays in our family were always a special occasion, as we gathered for good food and fellowship. Christmas was especially fun and plentiful in gifts.

Valedictorian of her class, speaking in front of a crowd never intimidated Patty Jo, nor did anything in life. She was one of a kind, special in every way. Church was also a great part of Patty Jo's life. Patty Jo was raised in the fellowship of Sandy Cross Baptist Church, where her mother played the piano for years, her father was a Deacon for a short time and even her grandmother led a choir. Talented in many areas of music, Patty Jo followed in the footsteps of her mother and grandmother. She was gifted in singing, leading, and playing multiple instruments. After completing the course work required by the Gates County School system, Patty Jo left Gates County and attended Meredith College where she majored in music and had planned to become a music teacher.

While in college, and being rooted deep in her relationship with God, Patty Jo found a local church to attend and of course just as it had been throughout the entirety of her life, she fit in and it was not long before she was leading the choir. She loved her new church family and often would write home about the friends she had made and how they had formed a bond and become her family away from home.

A few months after taking on the role of choir director, a young man by the name of Eugene "Rick" Pulley started attending the church and joined the choir. Patty Jo and Rick became acquainted and were smitten with one another almost instantly. It did not take long for Patty Jo to fall head over heels in love with Rick and brought him home to meet the family. I, myself, although young at the time, remember when she first brought him to meet us. I thought he was odd looking and laughed at his appearance at first glance.

After our first meeting with Rick, Patty Jo began to bring him home more often. Rick, an ordained minister, was outgoing, nice, funny, soft spoken and always willing to lend a helping hand. He also possessed talents that did not go unnoticed. It seemed that his ability to sing and play instruments was in sync with Patty Jo and they made the perfect team. It was not long before the two of them were engaged and on January 2nd1982 were married. Shortly after they married Patty Jo graduated from Meredith College with her degree in music education, not long after graduating, together, they were host of what was called "The Coffee House Ministry," an outreach program that catered to college students in the Raleigh, North Carolina, area.

After extending their ministry they were able to spread the word of God through contemporary Christian music for some years by traveling up and down the East Coast. Rick and Patty Jo often told us that pursuing many young people with their ministry was not always an easy task. Their challenge became a little tougher when they were called to Winston-Salem, North Carolina, to be the house parents, soon "mother" and "father," to twenty unwed and pregnant teenage girls, who desperately needed supervision and guidance.

In December 1985 the Winston-Salem Christian Center, which had supported Rick and Patty Jo and become their home base, announced its closing.

Rick and Patty Jo quickly remembered a church

they had visited outside of Danville, Virginia: Ringgold Christian Fellowship in the Sonshine Farm community. In February 1986 they moved to the Danville area, where they would continue the concert and retreat ministry. The transition from the small house in Winston-Salem, North Carolina, to the big, old farmhouse in the foothills of Danville proved to be a lovely interlude of significant change. In the Winter, the foothills are cold and often blanketed with snow and ice. In the Spring and summer temperatures are mild, and the pastures are green with vivid wildflowers. This is one of the reasons Rick and Patty Jo fell in love with the area.

They knew they would be surrounded by neighbors—church members, friends, acquaintances, and a welcoming Pastor—and were happy for their new opportunity. My family was happy for them and visited as often as we could, although it was not as often as we would have liked.

Patty Jo also talented in sewing and crafts made that old farmhouse her own. However, not long after moving their they began to struggle with the responsibility they had assumed. Rick's most time-consuming duty was to plan their road trips, which sometimes took them overseas to places such as Romania and Haiti. Patty Jo struggled because she carried the bulk of their responsibilities, which included writing some of the music they would later perform. In addition to singing many of the songs she wrote, Patty Jo helped Rick with the youth group and the coordination of plans and activities for their trips. Despite all her duties, Patty Jo managed to finish remodeling the large farmhouse and keep everything clean and tidy.

She never complained about her workload, but as the years passed, we detected that the stress was getting to her. The two of them were always helping others and had little free time just to be a couple. For a long time, Patty Jo spoke fondly of her best friend, Carrie, and her husband, who traveled with them for a few years as the other half of the retreat ministry. At some point it ended with the two couples going their separate ways. The split had its advantages in allowing Rick and Patty Jo to fulfill their longtime vision of providing an intensive Christian training program for teens.

They connected so well with the youth that they were sort of a second set of parents to certain teens for many years. Whenever the two of them could break away from their work, they would come home, mostly for holidays and special occasions. Whatever the event they always had an interesting story to share with the family. My family looked forward to Rick and Patty Jo coming home and were always sad when they had to leave. After being on the road for many years, traveling to share the gospel through word and music, Rick and Patty Jo made the decision to settle down and take over the youth group at their church.

The couple became heavily involved at the church and coming home was less frequent. After not seeing them for some time, when they did finally return home for a visit, Patty Jo had lost a tremendous amount of weight and become extremely thin. The two of them seemed happy, wherever one went—the other went. Rick never let Patty Jo get to far away from him. They displayed much love—one toward the other.

Mother's Day weekend in May 1999, Rick brought Patty Jo home to surprise her mom, and a surprise it was, they never came home for Mother's Day. The trip was short and unfortunately, I was not available to see them. Rick and Patty Jo left that Monday to return back to Ringgold and the following Saturday, May 15th 1999, my family received a call from Rick stating that Patty Jo was missing, he was with his Pastor and they had contacted the authorities.

Once my grandparents received word that Patty Jo was missing, they immediately contacted the rest of our family. We all met at my grandparent's home, to try and make sense out of what had happened. Arriving to my grandparent's house on that day was unsettling. Many different emotions flooded each of us, all at once. It was shocking and disheartening. We did not have cell phones, like we do now, and so we only had the one house phone and had to keep the line open in case Patty Jo called home.

As we waited, the phone would not stop ringing as everyone from neighbors, extended family, friends, and reporters called continuously. We quickly learned that when something of this magnitude happens the news spreads like a wildfire.

It was not long before Rick called us back and speaking to my grandfather informed him, that the truck Patty Jo had been driving, was found on a side road, not far from their house. According to Rick, Patty Jo had left to go shopping and was going to be returning home in time for them to leave and go to a play the youth at church were participating in at a local school.

Rick said, he waited, but Patty Jo never returned home.

He became really concerned the later it got and reached out to their Pastor who lived beside them, and they began searching for Patty Jo, before finally calling the Police to report her missing. My family and I concerned about Rick, decided that we should go and be with him.

Rick's family consisted of his mother, who lived in Raleigh, N.C., and us. Planning to leave first thing the next morning, to make the four-hour trip to Danville, Virginia, we decided who would go and who would stay with my grandparents. When we arrived the next day to the small Sonshine community, it was chaotic. There was a helicopter flying over, people were scattered everywhere, some of the church members and neighbors stood in front of the church, and others were walking the wooded area behind the parsonage—It was a lot to take in. We were not welcomed by the people and we noticed a young man was sitting on the steps blocking the entrance to Rick and Patty Jo's home.

We went and ask him where Rick was, we just wanted to get to Rick, hug him, and let him know we were all in this together. The young man informed us that Rick was being questioned by investigators and should not be much longer. After a few minutes I saw the investigators come out. They introduced themselves to us and handed us business cards, reassuring us that they were doing all they could to find Patty Jo. We ask if we could see Rick, they told us that he would be out momentarily.

When Rick came out of the house, we ran toward him to hug him and let him know we were there. I was the first one to reach him and when I looked at his face, I immediately noticed scratch marks on his right cheek. I ask Rick how he got the scratches. He stated that their dog, Grace had gotten away from him and ran into the woods behind their house and some briars got him. A Criminal Justice Major at the time, and having assisted on many investigations, I knew the scratches on his face were not briar scratches, but then I could not help thinking, why Rick would lie.

Desperate for answers we had flyers printed with a description of Patty Jo, along with her picture. My family and I made several trips to Danville. We met with Law Enforcement officers as much as we could. Every effort was put forth to try and find Patty Jo, including sending divers into local ponds and rivers, but each time, the answer was the same, officers had run into a dead end. The days turned to months and months to years as we went day after day with our minds on Patty Jo every minute.

We never gave up hope that Patty Jo may call, but hope grew dim as time passed. Throughout that time, whenever human remains were found, we would have to wait for the results from dental comparisons to see if it were Patty Jo. You do not realize how often human remains are found, until you go through that process.

Three and half years had passed, the holidays were once again approaching, and we still did not know Patty Jo's whereabouts. Rick had a yard sale and sold most of her belongings, the rest he gave to goodwill. He moved to Lebanon, Virginia and had become the only suspect in Patty Jo's disappearance. Finally, on December 18[th]2002 the lead investigator that I had maintained contact with, emailed me to let me know human remains had been found under the Hyco Creek bridge in Caswell County, North Carolina. The state was at the bridge preparing to tear it down and put up a new bridge, when one of the guys noticed, bones that appeared to be human remains. He immediately called the Caswell County Sheriff's Department who contacted the investigators in Danville, Virginia working the case.

The email read that they were waiting for the results from the dental comparison. I had read many emails and been through this several times, but this time was different. Somehow this time I knew it was Patty Jo. Within a few hours the investigator called me and said it was a match and they were going to arrest Rick. On December 26th 2002, we had Patty Jo's funeral. There were hundreds of people at the funeral, including the news media. Rick had yet to be arrested, and if he was at the funeral, we had no knowledge of it.

My family finally had closure and could rest well at night knowing Patty Jo was safe in the arms of Jesus. Rick was arrested and charged with First Degree murder and because Patty Jo was found in Caswell County, North Carolina, they had jurisdiction and that is where the trial was held. We spent months commuting to Caswell County to meet with the District Attorney and investigators. Once we had a trial date, we made all the necessary preparations, marking the days off our calendars, we anxiously awaited our day in court.

The mixture of excitement and nervousness dissipated when the District Attorney's office called to tell us the trial date had been postponed due to new evidence. We tried to remain rational, however that postponement turned out to be one of three. By the third postponement, we were beginning to wonder if the trial would ever take place.

After waiting for so long, once the trial began on October 19th 2004, we thought it would never end. We listened as witnesses testified giving a description of Rick that we never knew existed. In addition, we learned that Rick was controlling, had physically abused Patty Jo for the entirety of their marriage, had numerous affairs, he had an addiction to pornography, was abused as a child to the degree that his stepfather killed his pet rabbit and made him eat it for dinner one night. As an adult, he had become out of control. Their church family noticed incidents that did not add up, but no one said anything. We watched as they showed footage of Patty Jo's remains spread out on a table at the coroner's office. It was the most painful time of our lives. After nine long and emotionally draining days, a jury found Rick guilty of first-degree murder and he was sentenced to life without parole. Rick is currently still being housed in prison.

Patty Jo was an amazingly talented, loving, and giving person. All who met her, soon loved her. With a unique aura of peace and serenity about her, she appropriately spent many years serving the church. Nothing made her happier than honoring God by singing, writing music, and being the best example of a Christian that she could be each day. Unfortunately, she was too giving and understanding, too accepting of what she considered to be her destiny. Worst of all, she was fearful of failure, both too proud and ashamed to admit defeat, too hard working and able to cope, and too quiet about her life behind closed doors. All those qualities combined enabled Patty Jo to be a talented actress who would not let family and friends know her true needs.

Patty Jo disappeared and died many years before she should have. Secrets, selfishness, sickness, and lies killed her. In a way, it could be said that her entire adult life away from the core of her family was a mystery. Piece by painful piece, that mystery slowly came to light in quiet moments of faith between her disappearance and the discovery of her body. Although, we eventually acquired many facts about her life, disappearance, and death, our hearts will never truly comprehend all that contributed to the painful mystery that changed our lives forever. The nightmare my family lived through could have been avoided if someone, including Patty Jo, had not kept silent. If you are a victim of Domestic Violence or know someone who is, please speak out and take the appropriate measures to get help—silence kills, and no one should have to suffer the pain my family endured at the hands of a once abused child—turned victimizer.

CHAPTER FIVE

ENDING VIOLENCE
GODS WAY

DOMESTIC VIOLENCE IS WIDESPREAD and can affect anyone. However, some groups are more likely to be victims, as well as perpetrators. Women are most likely to be victims of abuse and perpetrators are most likely to be men. Children are often the hidden victims of Domestic Violence and abuse. Characteristics of a child's exposure to abuse or neglect have been shown to influence the risk for problematic outcomes.

Such characteristics include the point within the course of a child's development at which an experience of abuse or neglect occurs. There is evidence that childhood abuse increases the risk for crime and delinquency. A number of large prospective investigations in different parts of the United States have documented a relationship between childhood abuse and neglect and juvenile and/or adult crime (English et al.,2002)

Maxfield and Widom (1996) found that abuse and neglect experienced in childhood predicted violence and arrests in early adulthood. Adults with a history of abuse and neglect were more likely than adults without such a history to have committed nontraffic offenses (49 percent verses 38 percent) and violent crimes (18 percent verses 14 percent). Victims of childhood physical abuse and neglect were more likely to be arrested for violence, including Domestic Violence. Having worked as a Child Protective Service Investigator and working with victims of Domestic Violence, I witnessed how child abuse and Domestic Violence go hand in hand. With the exception, of a few parents who had a substance abuse addiction, most of the adults I worked with had been abused as children or witnessed violence in their home during their childhood.

While we often think of incidents of abuse occurring in homes where God is not a factor, the truth of the matter is, it is much more prominent in the homes of Christians than we would like to admit. Domestic Violence is an act of sin that is widespread and needs to be addressed from behind the pulpit. The perpetrators of this sin are in bondage with anger that has taken root and stems from a much deeper issue, most likely childhood abuse.

Satan has come to steal, kill, and destroy. Christian families are number one on his hit list. When a Christian family falls prey to the sin of violence, it allows Satan to have his way in their home, and eventually it makes its way into the church, as the violence is exposed. Once this problem is made known within the church, it can bring division if not handled properly, we then have division, not only in the home, but in the church as well. As the church goes—so goes the Nation.

Violence in the Christian family carries a domino effect. Given the opportunity it will destroy everything in its path. Fortunately, there is a remedy, and His name is Jesus. Jesus paid the price for victims of Domestic Violence, as well as perpetrators of Domestic Violence. Isaiah 53 tells us *"He is despised and rejected of men; a man of sorrows and acquainted with grief: and we hid as it were our faces from him; He was despised, and we esteemed Him not." (4) "Surely He has borne our griefs and carried our sorrows: yet we did esteem Him stricken, smitten of God, and afflicted." (5) "But He was wounded for our transgressions, He was bruised for our iniquities: the chastisement of our peace was upon Him; and with His stripes we are healed." (6) "All we like sheep have gone astray; we have turned everyone to his own way; and the Lord has laid on Him the iniquity of us all." (7) "He was oppressed, and He was afflicted, yet he opened not His mouth: He is brought as a lamb to the slaughter, and as a sheep before her shearers is dumb, so He opens not His mouth." (8) "He was taken from prison and from judgment: and who shall declare His generation? For He was cut off out of the land of the living for the transgressions of my people was He stricken." (9) And He made His grave with the wicked, and with the rich in His death; because He had done no violence, neither was any deceit in His mouth." (10) "Yet it pleased the Lord to bruise Him He has put Him to grief: when you shall make His soul an offering for sin, He shall see His seed, He shall prolong His days, and the pleasure of the Lord shall prosper in His hand." (11) "He shall see of the travail of His soul and shall be satisfied: by His knowledge shall My righteous servant justify many; for He shall bear their iniquities."*

God knows our sorrows, He is the healer of broken hearts, He sets at liberty those who are bruised, He sets the captive free. Jesus paid the price for all to be not only set free from sin but delivered from the bondages of darkness, that so easily besets us. Jesus is the solution for the abuse problem. To be a part of a church is to be a part of a family. Together we are members of God's household, or God's family.

God established believers to be connected in a powerful way as a family. To say that we are a church family implies the significant spiritual bond between believers, and the way we walk with one another through life, encouraging, supporting, praying, and loving each other. At the same time the church should be a safe haven, a place where victims of violence can break their silence, and reach out for help, without having to fear negative consequences or be made to feel like they have either done something wrong, or will be doing the unthinkable by leaving a marriage that has proven to be nothing but hurtful, physically and emotionally.

No one benefits, when bad advice is given based on scripture that has been taken out of context. Keep an open mind, follow the proper protocol and make it known to the congregation that living in violence is not a necessity, they do not have to keep silent, but there is an open door always available for them to walk through. If victims feel safe, and as if they can have their voice heard, then they are more likely to break the silence and enter in a lifestyle of freedom, whereby they can start to identify as a survivor. It is time the church—be the church—break the silence, I know first-hand how silence kills.

CHAPTER SIX

REPORTING ABUSE
AND NEGLECT

IT HAS BEEN PROVEN through many different studies that children who suffer abuse or neglect or witness Domestic Violence in the home are more likely to grow up and become perpetrators of violence as an adult. It is important that, not only, Police Officers, Doctors, Social Workers, Teachers, and the general public understand their duty to report suspected child abuse and neglect, but also Pastors and church leaders. Throughout this chapter I will be discussing the law concerning reporting abuse and neglect and maltreatment as well as what to expect once a report is filed with the local Department of Social Services.

In North Carolina there is a reporting law. The reporting law applies to any person or institution who has cause to suspect that any juvenile is abused, neglected, or dependent, as defined by G.S. 7B-101, or has died as the result of maltreatment to make a report to their local Department of Social Services. Mandated reporters are considered to be doctors, social workers, therapists, teachers, law enforcement officers and others whose professions sometimes involve them directly with problems of abuse, neglect, or dependency. Whether the person making the report has a professional or personal relationship with the child or the child's family, the relationship should not be grounds for delaying filing a report.

The reporting law does not permit anyone—professional, friend, or relative—to make an agreement not to report in exchange for an assurance that the person who may be responsible for a child's being abused, neglected, or dependent will seek help or take other action. A religious official, like everyone else, has a duty to report regardless of that official's relationship to the child.

North Carolina law relating to the competence of witnesses to testify in court has long recognized a clergy—communication privilege. Unlike most other statutory privileges, the clergy—communication privilege statute includes neither an exception for child abuse and neglect cases nor authority for the court to compel disclosure upon finding that disclosure is necessary to a proper administration of justice.

Before July 1,1999, the Juvenile Code explicitly overrode certain specified privileges, including husband—wife and doctor—patient but not the clergy—communication privilege. Since that time, however, the Code has provided unequivocally that no privilege, except a narrow attorney—client privilege, is grounds for failing to report suspected abuse, neglect, or dependency or for excluding evidence in a case involving the abuse, neglect, or dependency of a child.

If you suspect abuse or neglect the first step is to file a report with the Department of Social Services in the County where the child resides or is found. A report may be made in person, by telephone, or in writing. You do not have to identify yourself if you wish to remain anonymous. If you find yourself in a position to make a report after hours, the Department of Social Services has an after hours on call Social Worker, who is generally contacted by law enforcement. Therefore, all after hour calls should made to your local Sheriff or Police Department.

Once you have made contact, with the Department of Social Services a series of questions will be ask of you. It is vital that you have the following information:

1. The child's name, age, and address;
2. The name and address of the child's parent, guardian, custodian, or caretaker;
3. The names and ages of other children in the home;
4. The child's location if the child is not at the home address;
5. The nature and extent of any injury or condition resulting from abuse, neglect, or dependency; and
6. Any other information that might help establish the need for protective services or court intervention.

The information provided is held in strictest of confidence. The Social Worker after gathering all the information needed, will visit the child's home, and conduct and investigation or assessment, depending on the type of abuse or neglect. The Social Worker has a period of time to complete and finalize the investigation or assessment and once a decision is made regarding the case, he or she will notify the family as well as the reporter, informing them of their findings. If you remain anonymous, you will not receive this notification.

Reporting suspected child abuse or neglect can be the beginning of helping a child who is living in a home where violence is the norm. In the state of North Carolina even if a child is not being abused or neglected but resides in a home where domestic violence is occurring, it is mandated that a report be made to the Department of Social Services.

Unfortunately, this is oftentimes the only way Domestic Violence gets reported, and the only time a professional has the opportunity, to get involved. Domestic Violence is a type of abuse that only gets disclosed when the victim comes forth and tells someone. It is my opinion that, Domestic Violence should be made a part of Adult Protective Services, so that not only are the elderly protected, but victims of Domestic Violence as well. If we do all we can to intervene in the lives of children today, then perhaps they will develop into men and women who do not seek attention in the wrong places and who do not create violent homes in the future.

KNOW YOUR RIGHTS—
NORTH CAROLINA DOMESTIC
VIOLENCE LAWS

IT IS CRUCIAL THAT victims of Domestic Violence as well as those who find themselves in a position of trying to assist victims know the Laws surrounding Domestic Violence. The General Statutes contained in this chapter are for North Carolina only, other state laws may differ.

Chapter 50B. Domestic Violence.
§ 50B-1. Domestic violence; definition.

(a) Domestic violence means the commission of one or more of the following acts upon an aggrieved party or upon a minor child residing with or in the custody of the aggrieved party by a person with whom the aggrieved party has or has had a personal relationship, but does not include acts of self-defense:

(1) Attempting to cause bodily injury, or intentionally causing bodily injury; or
(2) Placing the aggrieved party or a member of the aggrieved party's family or household in fear of imminent serious bodily injury or continued

harassment, as defined in G.S. 14-277.3A, that rises to such a level as to inflict substantial emotional distress; or

(3) Committing any act defined in G.S. 14-27.21 through G.S. 14-27.33.

(b) For purposes of this section, the term "personal relationship" means a relationship wherein the parties involved:

(1) Are current or former spouses;

(2) Are persons of opposite sex who live together or have lived together;

(3) Are related as parents and children, including others acting in loco parentis to a minor child, or as grandparents and grandchildren. For purposes of this subdivision, an aggrieved party may not obtain an order of protection against a child or grandchild under the age of 16;

(4) Have a child in common;

(5) Are current or former household members;

(6) Are persons of the opposite sex who are in a dating relationship or have been in a dating relationship. For purposes of this subdivision, a dating relationship is one wherein the parties are romantically involved over time and on a continuous basis during the course of the relationship. A casual acquaintance or ordinary fraternization between persons in a business or social context is not a dating relationship.

(c) As used in this Chapter, the term "protective order" includes any order entered pursuant to this Chapter upon hearing by the court or consent of the parties. (1979, c. 561, s. 1; 1985, c. 113, s. 1; 1987, c. 828; 1987 (Reg. Sess., 1988), c. 893, ss. 1, 3; 1995 (Reg. Sess., 1996), c. 591, s. 1; 1997-471, s. 1; 2001-518, s. 3; 2003-107, s. 1; 2009-58, s. 5; 2015-181, s. 36

§ 50B-2. Institution of civil action; motion for emergency relief; temporary orders; temporary custody.

(a) Any person residing in this State may seek relief under this Chapter by filing a civil action or by filing a motion in any existing action filed under Chapter 50 of the General Statutes alleging acts of domestic violence against himself or herself or a minor child who resides with or is in the custody of such person. Any aggrieved party entitled to relief under this Chapter may file a civil action and proceed pro se, without the assistance of legal counsel. The district court division of the General Court of Justice shall have original jurisdiction over actions instituted under this Chapter. Any action for a domestic violence protective order requires that a summons be issued and served. The summons issued pursuant to this Chapter shall require the defendant to answer within 10 days of the date of service. Attachments to the summons shall include the complaint, notice of hearing, any temporary or ex parte order that has been issued, and other papers through the appropriate law enforcement agency where the defendant is to be served. In compliance with the federal Violence Against Women

Act, no court costs or attorneys' fees shall be assessed for the filing, issuance, registration, or service of a protective order or petition for a protective order or witness subpoena, except as provided in G.S. 1A-1, Rule 11.

(b) Emergency Relief. – A party may move the court for emergency relief if he or she believes there is a danger of serious and immediate injury to himself or herself or a minor child. A hearing on a motion for emergency relief, where no ex parte order is entered, shall be held after five days' notice of the hearing to the other party or after five days from the date of service of process on the other party, whichever occurs first, provided, however, that no hearing shall be required if the service of process is not completed on the other party. If the party is proceeding pro se and does not request an ex parte hearing, the clerk shall set a date for hearing and issue a notice of hearing within the time periods provided in this subsection, and shall effect service of the summons, complaint, notice, and other papers through the appropriate law enforcement agency where the defendant is to be served.

(c) Ex Parte Orders. –

(1) Prior to the hearing, if it clearly appears to the court from specific facts shown, that there is a danger of acts of domestic violence against the aggrieved party or a minor child, the court may enter orders as it deems necessary to protect the aggrieved party or minor children from those acts.

(2) A temporary order for custody ex parte and prior to service of process and notice shall not be entered unless the court finds that the child is exposed to a substantial risk of physical or emotional injury or sexual abuse.

(3) If the court finds that the child is exposed to a substantial risk of physical or emotional injury or sexual abuse, upon request of the aggrieved party, the court shall consider and may order the other party to (i) stay away from a minor child, or (ii) return a minor child to, or not remove a minor child from, the physical care of a parent or person in loco parentis, if the court finds that the order is in the best interest of the minor child and is necessary for the safety of the minor child.

(4) If the court determines that it is in the best interest of the minor child for the other party to have contact with the minor child or children, the court shall issue an order designed to protect the safety and well-being of the minor child and the aggrieved party. The order shall specify the terms of contact between the other party and the minor child and may include a specific schedule of time and location of exchange of the minor child, supervision by a third party or supervised visitation center, and any other conditions that will ensure both the well-being of the minor child and the aggrieved party.

(5) Upon the issuance of an ex parte order under this subsection, a hearing shall be held within 10 days

from the date of issuance of the order or within seven days from the date of service of process on the other party, whichever occurs later. A continuance shall be limited to one extension of no more than 10 days unless all parties consent or good cause is shown. The hearing shall have priority on the court calendar.

(6) If an aggrieved party acting pro se requests ex parte relief, the clerk of superior court shall schedule an ex parte hearing with the district court division of the General Court of Justice within 72 hours of the filing for said relief, or by the end of the next day on which the district court is in session in the county in which the action was filed, whichever shall first occur. If the district court is not in session in said county, the aggrieved party may contact the clerk of superior court in any other county within the same judicial district who shall schedule an ex parte hearing with the district court division of the General Court of Justice by the end of the next day on which said court division is in session in that county.

(7) Upon the issuance of an ex parte order under this subsection, if the party is proceeding pro se, the Clerk shall set a date for hearing and issue a notice of hearing within the time periods provided in this subsection, and shall effect service of the summons, complaint, notice, order and other papers through the appropriate law enforcement agency where the defendant is to be served.

(c1) Ex Parte Orders by Authorized Magistrate. – The chief district court judge may authorize a magistrate or magistrates to hear any motions for emergency relief ex parte. Prior to the hearing, if the magistrate determines that at the time the party is seeking emergency relief ex parte the district court is not in session and a district court judge is not and will not be available to hear the motion for a period of four or more hours, the motion may be heard by the magistrate. If it clearly appears to the magistrate from specific facts shown that there is a danger of acts of domestic violence against the aggrieved party or a minor child, the magistrate may enter orders as it deems necessary to protect the aggrieved party or minor children from those acts, except that a temporary order for custody ex parte and prior to service of process and notice shall not be entered unless the magistrate finds that the child is exposed to a substantial risk of physical or emotional injury or sexual abuse. If the magistrate finds that the child is exposed to a substantial risk of physical or emotional injury or sexual abuse, upon request of the aggrieved party, the magistrate shall consider and may order the other party to stay away from a minor child, or to return a minor child to, or not remove a minor child from, the physical care of a parent or person in loco parentis, if the magistrate finds that the order is in the best interest of the minor child and is necessary for the safety of the minor child. If the magistrate determines that it is in the best interest of the minor child for the other party to have contact with the minor child or children, the magistrate shall issue an order designed to protect the safety and well-being of the minor child and the aggrieved party. The order shall specify the terms of contact between the other party and the minor child and may include a specific schedule of time and location of exchange of the minor child, supervision by a third party or supervised visitation center, and any other conditions that will ensure both the well-being of the minor child and the aggrieved party. An ex parte order entered under this subsection shall expire and the magistrate shall schedule an ex parte hearing before a district court judge by the end of the next day on which the district court is in session in the county in which the action was filed. Ex parte orders entered by the district court judge pursuant to this subsection shall be entered and scheduled in accordance with subsection (c) of this section.

(c2) The authority granted to authorized magistrates to award temporary child custody pursuant to subsection (c1) of this section and pursuant to G.S. 50B-3(a)(4) is granted subject to custody rules to be established by the supervising chief district judge of each judicial district.

(d) Pro Se Forms. – The clerk of superior court of each county shall provide to pro se complainants all forms that are necessary or appropriate to enable them to proceed pro se pursuant to this section. The clerk shall, whenever feasible, provide a private area for complainants to fill out forms and make inquiries. The clerk shall provide a supply of pro se forms to authorized magistrates who shall make the forms available to complainants seeking relief under subsection (c1) of this section.

(e) All documents filed, issued, registered, or served in an action under this Chapter relating to an ex parte, emergency, or permanent domestic violence protective order may be filed electronically. (1979, c. 561, s. 1; 1985, c. 113, ss. 2, 3; 1987 (Reg. Sess., 1988), c. 893, s. 2; 1989, c. 461, s. 1; 1994, Ex. Sess., c. 4, s. 1; 1997-471, s. 2; 2001-518, s. 4; 2002-126, s. 29A.6(a); 2004-186, ss. 17.2, 19.1; 2009-342, s. 2; 2012-20, s. 1; 2013-390, s. 1; 2015-62, s. 3(b); 2021-47.

§ 50B-3. Relief.

(a) If the court, including magistrates as authorized under G.S. 50B-2(c1), finds that an act of domestic violence has occurred, the court shall grant a protective order restraining the defendant from further acts of domestic violence. A protective order may include any of the following types of relief:

(1) Direct a party to refrain from such acts.
(2) Grant to a party possession of the residence or household of the parties and exclude the other party from the residence or household.
(3) Require a party to provide a spouse and his or her children suitable alternate housing.
(4) Award temporary custody of minor children and establish temporary visitation rights pursuant to G.S. 50B-2 if the order is granted ex parte, and pursuant to subsection (a1) of this section if the order is granted after notice or service of process.

(5) Order the eviction of a party from the residence or household and assistance to the victim in returning to it.

(6) Order either party to make payments for the support of a minor child as required by law.

(7) Order either party to make payments for the support of a spouse as required by law.

(8) Provide for possession of personal property of the parties, including the care, custody, and control of any animal owned, possessed, kept, or held as a pet by either party or minor child residing in the household.

(9) Order a party to refrain from doing any or all of the following:

   a. Threatening, abusing, or following the other party.

   b. Harassing the other party, including by telephone, visiting the home or workplace, or other means.

   b1. Cruelly treating or abusing an animal owned, possessed, kept, or held as a pet by either party or minor child residing in the household. c. Otherwise interfering with the other party.

(10) Award attorney's fees to either party.

(11) Prohibit a party from purchasing a firearm for a time fixed in the order.

(12) Order any party the court finds is responsible for acts of domestic violence to attend and complete

an abuser treatment program if the program is approved by the Domestic Violence Commission.

(13) Include any additional prohibitions or requirements the court deems necessary to protect any party or any minor child.

(a1) Upon the request of either party at a hearing after notice or service of process, the court shall consider and may award temporary custody of minor children and establish temporary visitation rights as follows:

(1) In awarding custody or visitation rights, the court shall base its decision on the best interest of the minor child with particular consideration given to the safety of the minor child.

(2) For purposes of determining custody and visitation issues, the court shall consider:

a. Whether the minor child was exposed to a substantial risk of physical or emotional injury or sexual abuse.

b. Whether the minor child was present during acts of domestic violence.

c. Whether a weapon was used or threatened to be used during any act of domestic violence.

d. Whether a party caused or attempted to cause serious bodily injury to the aggrieved party or the minor child.

e. Whether a party placed the aggrieved party or the minor child in reasonable fear of imminent serious bodily injury.

f. Whether a party caused an aggrieved party to engage involuntarily in sexual relations by force, threat, or duress.

g. Whether there is a pattern of abuse against an aggrieved party or the minor child.

h. Whether a party has abused or endangered the minor child during visitation.

i. Whether a party has used visitation as an opportunity to abuse or harass the aggrieved party.

j. Whether a party has improperly concealed or detained the minor child.

k. Whether a party has otherwise acted in a manner that is not in the best interest of the minor child.

(3) If the court awards custody, the court shall also consider whether visitation is in the best interest of the minor child. If ordering visitation, the court shall provide for the safety and well-being of the minor child and the safety of the aggrieved party. The court may consider any of the following:

a. Ordering an exchange of the minor child to occur in a protected setting or in the presence of an appropriate third party.

b. Ordering visitation supervised by an appropriate third party, or at a supervised visitation center or other approved agency.

c. Ordering the noncustodial parent to attend and complete, to the satisfaction of the court, an abuser treatment program as a condition of visitation.

d. Ordering either or both parents to abstain from possession or consumption of alcohol or controlled substances during the visitation or for 24 hours preceding an exchange of the minor child.

e. Ordering the noncustodial parent to pay the costs of supervised visitation.

f. Prohibiting overnight visitation.

g. Requiring a bond from the noncustodial parent for the return and safety of the minor child.

h. Ordering an investigation or appointment of a guardian ad litem or attorney for the minor child.

i. Imposing any other condition that is deemed necessary to provide for the safety and well-being of the minor child and the safety of the aggrieved party. If the court grants visitation, the order shall specify dates and times for the visitation to take place or other specific parameters or conditions that are appropriate. A person, supervised visitation center, or other agency may be approved to supervise visitation after appearing in court or filing an affidavit accepting that responsibility and acknowledging accountability to the court.

(4) A temporary custody order entered pursuant to this Chapter shall be without prejudice and shall

be for a fixed period of time not to exceed one year. Nothing in this section shall be construed to affect the right of the parties to a de novo hearing under Chapter 50 of the General Statutes.

(a2) If the court orders that the defendant attend an abuser treatment program pursuant to G.S. 50B-3(a)(12), the defendant shall begin regular attendance of the program within 60 days of the entry of the order. When ordering a defendant to attend an abuser treatment program, the court shall also specify a date and time for a review hearing with the court to assess whether the defendant has complied with that part of the order. The review hearing shall be held as soon as practicable after 60 days from the entry of the original order. The date of the review shall be set at the same time as the entry of the original order, and the clerk shall issue a Notice of Hearing for the compliance review to be given to the defendant and filed with the court on the same day as the entry of the order. If a defendant is not present in court at the time the order to attend an abuser treatment program is entered and the Notice of Hearing for review is filed, the clerk shall serve a copy of the Notice of Hearing together with the service of the order. The plaintiff may, but is not required to, attend the 60-day review hearing.

(a3) At any time prior to the 60-day review hearing set forth in subsection (a2) of this section, a defendant who is ordered to attend an abuser treatment program may present to the clerk a written statement from an abuser treatment program showing that the defendant has enrolled in and begun regular attendance in an abuser treatment program. Upon receipt of the written statement, the clerk shall remove the 60-day review hearing from the court docket, and the defendant shall not be required to appear for the 60-day review hearing. The clerk shall also notify the plaintiff that the defendant has complied with the order and that no 60-day review hearing will occur.

(b) Protective orders entered pursuant to this Chapter shall be for a fixed period of time not to exceed one year. The court may renew a protective order for a fixed period of time not to exceed two years, including an order that previously has been renewed, upon a motion by the aggrieved party filed before the expiration of the current order; provided, however, that a temporary award of custody entered as part of a protective order may not be renewed to extend a temporary award of custody beyond the maximum one-year period. The court may renew a protective order for good cause. The commission of an act as defined in G.S. 50B-1(a) by the defendant after entry of the current order is not required for an order to be renewed. Protective orders entered, including consent orders, shall not be mutual in nature except where both parties file a claim and the court makes detailed findings of fact indicating that both parties acted as aggressors, that neither party acted primarily in self-defense, and that the right of each party to due process is preserved. Protective orders entered pursuant to this Chapter expire at 11:59 P.M. on the indicated expiration date, unless specifically stated otherwise in the order.

(b1) A consent protective order may be entered pursuant to this Chapter without findings of fact and conclusions of law if the parties agree in writing that no findings of fact and conclusions of law will be included in the consent protective order. The consent protective order shall be valid and enforceable and shall have the same force and effect as a protective order entered with findings of fact and conclusions of law.

(b2) Upon the written request of either party at a hearing after notice or service of process, the court may modify any protective order entered pursuant to this Chapter after a finding of good cause.

(c) A copy of any order entered and filed under this Article shall be issued to each party. Law enforcement agencies shall accept receipt of copies of the order issued by the clerk of court by electronic or facsimile transmission for service on defendants. In addition, a copy of the order shall be issued promptly to and retained by the police department of the city of the victim's residence. If the victim does not reside in a city or resides in a city with no police department, copies shall be issued promptly to and retained by the sheriff, and the county police department, if any, of the county in which the victim resides. If the defendant is ordered to stay away from the child's school, a copy of the order shall be delivered promptly by the sheriff to the principal or, in the principal's absence, the assistant principal or the principal's designee of each school named in the order.

(c1) When a protective order issued under this Chapter is filed with the Clerk of Superior Court, the clerk shall provide to the applicant an informational sheet developed by the Administrative Office of the Courts that includes:

(1)   Domestic violence agencies and services.
(2)   Sexual assault agencies and services.
(3)   Victims' compensation services.
(4)   Legal aid services.
(5)   Address confidentiality services.
(6)   An explanation of the plaintiff's right to apply for a permit under G.S. 14-415.15.

(d) The sheriff of the county where a domestic violence order is entered shall provide for prompt entry of the order into the National Crime Information Center registry and shall provide for access of such orders to magistrates on a 24-hour-a-day basis. Modifications, terminations, renewals, and dismissals of the order shall also be promptly entered. (1979, c. 561, s. 1; 1985, c. 463; 1994, Ex. Sess., c. 4, s. 2; 1995, c. 527, s. 1; 1995 (Reg. Sess., 1996), c. 591, s. 2; c. 742, s. 42.1.; 1999-23, s. 1; 2000-125, s. 9; 2002-105, s. 2; 2002-126, s. 29A.6(b); 2003-107, s. 2; 2004-186, ss. 17.3-17.5; 2005-343, s. 2; 2005-423, s. 1; 2007-116, s. 3; 2009-425, s. 1; 2013-237, s. 1; 2015-176, s. 1; 2017-92, s. 2; 2019-168, ss. 1, 2(b).)

§ 50B-3.1. Surrender and disposal of firearms; violations; exemptions.

(a) Required Surrender of Firearms. – Upon issuance of an emergency or ex parte order pursuant to this Chapter, the court shall order the defendant to surrender to the sheriff all firearms, machine guns, ammunition, permits to purchase firearms, and permits to carry concealed firearms that are in the care, custody, possession, ownership, or control of the defendant if the court finds any of the following factors:

(1) The use or threatened use of a deadly weapon by the defendant or a pattern of prior conduct involving the use or threatened use of violence with a firearm against persons.

(2) Threats to seriously injure or kill the aggrieved party or minor child by the defendant.

(3) Threats to commit suicide by the defendant.

(4) Serious injuries inflicted upon the aggrieved party or minor child by the defendant.

(b) Ex Parte or Emergency Hearing. – The court shall inquire of the plaintiff, at the ex parte or emergency hearing, the presence of, ownership of, or otherwise access to firearms by the defendant, as well as ammunition, permits to purchase firearms, and permits to carry concealed firearms, and include, whenever possible, identifying information regarding the description, number, and location of firearms, ammunition, and permits in the order.

(c) Ten-Day Hearing. – The court, at the 10-day hearing, shall inquire of the defendant the presence of, ownership of, or otherwise access to firearms by the defendant, as well as ammunition, permits to purchase firearms, and permits to carry concealed firearms, and include, whenever possible, identifying information regarding the description, number, and location of firearms, ammunition, and permits in the order.

(d) Surrender. – Upon service of the order, the defendant shall immediately surrender to the sheriff possession of all firearms, machine guns, ammunition, permits to purchase firearms, and permits to carry concealed firearms that are in the care, custody, possession, ownership, or control of the defendant. In the event that weapons cannot be surrendered at the time the order is served, the defendant shall surrender the firearms, ammunitions, and permits to the sheriff within 24 hours of service at a time and place specified by the sheriff. The sheriff shall store the firearms or contract with a licensed firearms dealer to provide storage.

(1) If the court orders the defendant to surrender firearms, ammunition, and permits, the court shall inform the plaintiff and the defendant of the terms of the protective order and include these terms on the face of the order, including that the defendant is prohibited from possessing, purchasing, or receiving or attempting to possess, purchase, or receive a firearm for so long as the protective order or any successive protective order is in effect. The terms of the order shall include instructions as to how the defendant may request retrieval of any firearms, ammunition, and permits surrendered to the sheriff when the protective order is no longer

in effect. The terms shall also include notice of the penalty for violation of G.S. 14-269.8.

(2) The sheriff may charge the defendant a reasonable fee for the storage of any firearms and ammunition taken pursuant to a protective order. The fees are payable to the sheriff. The sheriff shall transmit the proceeds of these fees to the county finance officer. The fees shall be used by the sheriff to pay the costs of administering this section and for other law enforcement purposes. The county shall expend the restricted funds for these purposes only. The sheriff shall not release firearms, ammunition, or permits without a court order granting the release. The defendant must remit all fees owed prior to the authorized return of any firearms, ammunition, or permits. The sheriff shall not incur any civil or criminal liability for alleged damage or deterioration due to storage or transportation of any firearms or ammunition held pursuant to this section.

(e) Retrieval. – If the court does not enter a protective order when the ex parte or emergency order expires, the defendant may retrieve any weapons surrendered to the sheriff unless the court finds that the defendant is precluded from owning or possessing a firearm pursuant to State or federal law or final disposition of any pending criminal charges committed against the person that is the subject of the current protective order.

(f) Motion for Return. – The defendant may request the return of any firearms, ammunition, or permits surrendered by filing a motion with the court at the expiration of the current order or final disposition of any pending criminal charges committed against the person that is the subject of the current protective order and not later than 90 days after the expiration of the current order or final disposition of any pending criminal charges committed against the person that is the subject of the current protective order. Upon receipt of the motion, the court shall schedule a hearing and provide written notice to the plaintiff who shall have the right to appear and be heard and to the sheriff who has control of the firearms, ammunition, or permits. The court shall determine whether the defendant is subject to any State or federal law or court order that precludes the defendant from owning or possessing a firearm. The inquiry shall include:

(1) Whether the protective order has been renewed.

(2) Whether the defendant is subject to any other protective orders.

(3) Whether the defendant is disqualified from owning or possessing a firearm pursuant to 18 U.S.C. § 922 or any State law.

(4) Whether the defendant has any pending criminal charges, in either State or federal court, committed against the person that is the subject of the current protective order. The court shall deny the return of firearms, ammunition, or permits if the court finds that the defendant is precluded from owning

or possessing a firearm pursuant to State or federal law or if the defendant has any pending criminal charges, in either State or federal court, committed against the person that is the subject of the current protective order until the final disposition of those charges.

(g) Motion for Return by Third-Party Owner. – A third-party owner of firearms, ammunition, or permits who is otherwise eligible to possess such items may file a motion requesting the return to said third party of any such items in the possession of the sheriff seized as a result of the entry of a domestic violence protective order. The motion must be filed not later than 30 days after the seizure of the items by the sheriff. Upon receipt of the third party's motion, the court shall schedule a hearing and provide written notice to all parties and the sheriff. The court shall order return of the items to the third party unless the court determines that the third party is disqualified from owning or possessing said items pursuant to State or federal law. If the court denies the return of said items to the third party, the items shall be disposed of by the sheriff as provided in subsection (h) of this section.

(h) Disposal of Firearms. – If the defendant does not file a motion requesting the return of any firearms, ammunition, or permits surrendered within the time period prescribed by this section, if the court determines that the defendant is precluded from regaining possession of any firearms, ammunition, or permits surrendered, or if the defendant or third-party owner fails to remit all fees owed for the storage of the firearms or ammunition within 30 days of the entry of the order granting the return of the firearms, ammunition, or permits, the sheriff who has control of the firearms, ammunition, or permits shall give notice to the defendant, and the sheriff shall apply to the court for an order of disposition of the firearms, ammunition, or permits. The judge, after a hearing, may order the disposition of the firearms, ammunition, or permits in one or more of the ways authorized by law, including subdivision (4), (4b), (5), or (6) of G.S. 14-269.1. If a sale by the sheriff does occur, any proceeds from the sale after deducting any costs associated with the sale, and in accordance with all applicable State and federal law, shall be provided to the defendant, if requested by the defendant by motion made before the hearing or at the hearing and if ordered by the judge.

(i) It is unlawful for any person subject to a protective order prohibiting the possession or purchase of firearms to:

(1) Fail to surrender all firearms, ammunition, permits to purchase firearms, and permits to carry concealed firearms to the sheriff as ordered by the court;

(2) Fail to disclose all information pertaining to the possession of firearms, ammunition, and permits to purchase and permits to carry concealed firearms as requested by the court; or

(3) Provide false information to the court pertaining to any of these items.

(j) Violations. – In accordance with G.S. 14-269.8, it is unlawful for any person to possess, purchase, or receive or attempt to possess, purchase, or receive a firearm, as defined in G.S. 14-409.39(2), machine gun, ammunition, or permits to purchase or carry concealed firearms if ordered by the court for so long as that protective order or any successive protective order entered against that person pursuant to this Chapter is in effect. Any defendant violating the provisions of this section shall be guilty of a Class H felony.

(k) Official Use Exemption. – This section shall not prohibit law enforcement officers and members of any branch of the Armed Forces of the United States, not otherwise prohibited under federal law, from possessing or using firearms for official use only.

(l) Nothing in this section is intended to limit the discretion of the court in granting additional relief as provided in other sections of this Chapter. (2003-410, s. 1; 2004-203, s. 34(a); 2005-287, s. 4; 2005-423, ss. 2, 3; 2011-183, s. 40; 2011-268, ss. 23, 24.)

§ 50B-4. Enforcement of orders.

(a) A party may file a motion for contempt for violation of any order entered pursuant to this Chapter. This party may file and proceed with that motion pro se, using forms provided by the clerk of superior court or a magistrate authorized under G.S. 50B-2(c1). Upon the filing pro se of a motion for contempt under this subsection, the clerk, or the authorized magistrate, if the facts show clearly that there is danger of acts of domestic violence against the aggrieved party or a minor child and the motion is made at a time when the clerk is not available, shall schedule and issue notice of a show cause hearing with the district court division of the General Court of Justice at the earliest possible date pursuant to G.S. 5A-23. The Clerk, or the magistrate in the case of notice issued by the magistrate pursuant to this subsection, shall effect service of the motion, notice, and other papers through the appropriate law enforcement agency where the defendant is to be served.

(a) Repealed by Session Laws 1999-23, s. 2, effective February 1, 2000.

(b) A valid protective order entered pursuant to this Chapter shall be enforced by all North Carolina law enforcement agencies without further order of the court.

(c) A valid protective order entered by the courts of another state or the courts of an Indian tribe shall be accorded full faith and credit by the courts of North Carolina whether or not the order has been registered and shall be enforced by the courts and the law enforcement agencies of North Carolina as if it were an order issued by a North Carolina court. In determining the validity of an out-of-state order for purposes of enforcement, a law enforcement officer may rely upon a copy of the protective order issued by another state or the courts of an Indian tribe that is provided to the officer and on the statement of a person protected by the order that the order remains in effect. Even though registration is not required, a copy of a protective order may be registered in North Carolina by filing with the clerk of superior court in any county a copy of the order and an affidavit by a person protected by the order that to the best of that person's knowledge the order is presently in effect as written. Notice of the registration shall not be given to the defendant. Upon registration of the order, the clerk shall promptly forward a copy to the sheriff of that county. Unless the issuing state has already entered the order, the sheriff shall provide for prompt entry of the order into the National Crime Information Center registry pursuant to G.S. 50B-3(d).

(d) Upon application or motion by a party to the court, the court shall determine whether an out-of-state order remains in full force and effect.

(e) The term "valid protective order," as used in subsections (c) and (d) of this section, shall include an emergency or ex parte order entered under this Chapter. (g) Notwithstanding the provisions of G.S. 1-294, a valid protective order entered pursuant to this Chapter which has been appealed to the appellate division is enforceable in the trial court during the pendency of the appeal. Upon motion by the aggrieved party, the court of the appellate division in which the appeal is pending may stay an order of the trial court until the appeal is decided, if justice so requires. (1979, c. 561, s. 1; 1985, c. 113, s. 4; 1987, c. 739, s. 6; 1989, c. 461, s. 2; 1994, Ex. Sess., c. 4, s. 3; 1995

(Reg. Sess., 1996), c. 591, s. 3; 1999-23, ss. 2; 2002-126, s. 29A.6(c); 2003-107, s. 3; 2009-342, s. 4; 2017-92, s. 1.)

§ 50B-4.2. False statement regarding protective order a misdemeanor.

A person who knowingly makes a false statement to a law enforcement agency or officer that a protective order entered pursuant to this Chapter or by the courts of another state or Indian tribe remains in effect shall be guilty of a Class 2 misdemeanor. (1999-23, s. 5.)

§ 50B-5. Emergency assistance.

(a) A person who alleges that he or she or a minor child has been the victim of domestic violence may request the assistance of a local law enforcement agency. The local law enforcement agency shall respond to the request for assistance as soon as practicable. The local law enforcement officer responding to the request for assistance may take whatever steps are reasonably necessary to protect the complainant from harm and may advise the complainant of sources of shelter, medical care, counseling and other services. Upon request by the complainant and where feasible, the law enforcement officer may transport the complainant to appropriate facilities such as hospitals, magistrates' offices, or public or private facilities for shelter and accompany the complainant to his or her residence, within the jurisdiction in which the request for assistance was made, so that the complainant may remove food, clothing, medication and such other personal property as is reasonably necessary to enable the complainant and any minor children who are presently in the care of the complainant to remain elsewhere pending further proceedings.

(b) In providing the assistance authorized by subsection

(c), no officer may be held criminally or civilly liable on account of reasonable measures taken under authority of subsection (a). (1979, c. 561, s. 1; 1985, c. 113, s. 5; 1999-23, s. 6.)

§ 50B-5.5. Employment discrimination unlawful.

(a) No employer shall discharge, demote, deny a promotion, or discipline an employee because the employee took reasonable time off from work to obtain or attempt to obtain relief under this Chapter. An employee who is absent from the workplace shall follow the employer's usual time-off policy or procedure, including advance notice to the employer, when required by the employer's usual procedures, unless an emergency prevents the employee from doing so. An employer may require documentation of any emergency that prevented the employee from complying in advance with the employer's usual time-off policy or procedure, or any other information available to the employee which supports the employee's reason for being absent from the workplace.

(b) The Commissioner of Labor shall enforce the provisions of this section according to Article 21 of Chapter 95 of the General Statutes, including the rules and regulations issued pursuant to the Article. (2004-186, s. 18.1.)

§ 50B-6. Construction of Chapter. This Chapter shall not be construed as granting a status to any person for any purpose other than those expressly stated herein. This Chapter shall not be construed as relieving any person or institution of the duty to report to the department of social services, as required by G.S. 7B-301, if the person or institution has cause to suspect that a juvenile is abused or neglected. (1979, c. 561, s. 1; 1985, c. 113, s. 6; 1998-202, s. 13(r).)

§ 50B-7. Remedies not exclusive.

(a) The remedies provided by this Chapter are not exclusive but are additional to remedies provided under Chapter 50 and elsewhere in the General Statutes.

(b) Any subsequent court order entered supersedes similar provisions in protective issued pursuant to this Chapter. (1979, c. 561, s. 1; 2019-168, s. 2(a).)

§ 50B-8. Effect upon prosecution for violation of § 14-184 or other offense against public morals.

The granting of a protective order, prosecution for violation of this Chapter, or the granting of any other relief or the institution of any other enforcement proceedings under this Chapter shall not be construed to afford a defense to any person or persons charged with fornication and adultery under G.S. 14-184 or charged with any other offense against the public morals; and prosecution, conviction, or prosecution and conviction for violation of any provision of this Chapter shall not be a bar to prosecution for violation of G.S. 14-184 or of any other statute defining an offense or offenses against the public morals. (1979, c. 561, s. 1; 2003-107, s. 4.)

§ 50B-9. Domestic Violence Center Fund.

(a) The Domestic Violence Center Fund is established within the State Treasury. The fund shall be administered by the Department of Administration, North Carolina Council for Women and Youth Involvement, and shall be used to make grants to centers for victims of domestic violence and to The North Carolina Coalition Against Domestic Violence, Incorporated. This fund shall be administered in accordance with the provisions of the State Budget Act. The Department of Administration shall make quarterly grants to each eligible domestic violence center and to The North Carolina Coalition Against Domestic Violence, Incorporated. The Department of Administration shall send the contracts to grantees within 10 business days of the date the Current Operations Appropriations Act, as defined in G.S. 143C-1-1, is certified for that fiscal year.

(b) Each grant recipient shall receive the same amount. To be eligible to receive funds under this section, a domestic violence center must meet the following requirements:

(1) It shall have been in operation on the preceding July 1 and shall continue to be in operation.

(2) It shall offer all of the following services: a hotline, transportation services, community education programs, daytime services, and call forwarding during the night and it shall fulfill other criteria established by the Department of Administration.

(3) It shall be a nonprofit corporation or a local governmental entity.

(c) On or before September 1, the North Carolina Council for Women and Youth Involvement shall report on the quarterly distributions of the grants from the Domestic Violence Center Fund to the House and Senate chairs of the General Government Appropriations Committee and the Fiscal Research Division. The report shall include the following:

(1) Date, amount, and recipients of the fund disbursements.

(2) Eligible programs which are ineligible to receive funding during the relative reporting cycle as well as the reason of the ineligibility for that relative reporting cycle. (1991, c. 693, s. 3; 1991 (Reg. Sess., 1992), c. 988, s. 1; 2017-57, s. 31.2(a); 2021-180, s. 20.6(a).)

ENCOURAGING WORDS FOR VICTIMS AND SURVIVORS

ANGER HAS BEEN MANIFESTING in man, resulting in violence being displayed in families, since the beginning of time, when Cain murdered his brother, Abel. However, God says that we are to love one another, not as Cain, who was of that wicked one, and slew his brother, but as God loves us, so much that He gave His son. (I John 3, KJV)

Men are called by God to love their wives as their own bodies and women are to love their husbands and submit to them as unto the Lord, providing they are both Christians and their relationship is healthy and strong.

At times in Christian homes these scriptures are used out of context and for the purpose of gaining control, one over the other, as well, some Pastors and others in leadership, do the same and encourage women to stay in an abusive marriage, where their life is being placed at risk. This is not what God intended for marriage, furthermore, what is being portrayed by the parents and witnessed by children in the home, unfortunately, more times than not, gets embedded into the child so deeply, that as adults they to, become perpetrators of violence.

In the eyes of God, violence whether it be, Domestic

Violence or child abuse, is sin. God is not pleased with acts of violence brought against His children, nor does He want His children living in bondage with a Spirit of anger. While there are many avenues one may take to get help with anger or as a victim, to learn techniques in coping and being educated on what to look for, what to do and knowing their rights, there is only one solution to the problem of violence in the home and His name is Jesus.

Whether a current victim of Domestic Violence or a survivor of such violence, the remainder of this book is filled with Gods word, followed by a short devotion to encourage and aid in healing and growing closer to God, while moving further away from the long existing effects caused by living a life of abuse.

It is my prayer that victims be comforted, healed, and set free, as well, I pray perpetrators of this erroneous act of sin be delivered from the root cause of anger that so easily controls them. May we all work together to end the silent cry of those who feel they have no one to turn to for help and be a support, they can trust and rely upon. The silence must be broken—lives are at stake—silence kills.

"Come unto me, all you who labor and are heavy laden, and I will give you rest."

-Matthew 11:28

Are You Exhausted?

A RE YOU EXHAUSTED? WE all have circumstance that we are wrestling with as we go about our daily lives. Physically, we grow tired from the activities that pull at us throughout the day. We can eat healthy and get an ample amount of sleep to maintain our bodies, but physical exhaustion is inevitable. Mentally, we tend to become drained from our own thoughts and worry, not to mention, the pull of our friends, coworkers, and family who rely on us for a sound word of advice in their time of trouble.

While we can an encouragement to one another, our words of encouragement and acts of kindness can only go so far. We can cheer a person up, but we cannot bring them to a place of rest. True rest comes from God. So, how do we obtain the rest of God? By taking every burden, whether it be physical, mental, or something else, and laying it at the foot of the cross. We surrender it all and say "Lord, I do not have the means to do this, but you do." In doing so, we cease with our own efforts, which wear us down, and we trust God, by faith, to resolve the problems as only He can do. While He is working—we rest.

Be encouraged today to stop worrying over situations you cannot change and laboring to force an outcome that will, most likely, only make things worse. Rest in the arms of Jesus. He NEVER disappoints—He's got you—Just rest.

Meditations

_____

_____

_____

_____

_____

_____

_____

_____

_____

_____

_____

_____

_____

_____

_____

_____

_____

_____

_____

_____

_____

_____

*"The Lord will give strength unto his people; the
Lord will bless his people with peace."*

-Psalm 29:11

Our Strength

ONE SUNDAY DURING OUR morning worship service, the Lord gave my Pastor a word for the congregation and that word was "GET UP!" How do we "GET UP" when the troubles of this life are weighing us down? How do we "GET UP" when things like abuse, depression, anxiety, addiction, broken relationships, financial burdens, poor health, and difficulties on the job are binding, refusing to let go, no matter our efforts?

How do we "GET UP?" We "GET UP" by exchanging our efforts for Gods strength. We must learn to rest and maintain our faith in Christ Jesus. He alone is our strength, refuge, help and peace. He defeated EVERY trouble we face today at Calvary's Cross of yesterday. Whatever you are dealing with, no matter how significant or insignificant it may seem, release it to your Father in Heaven.

He is faithful to perform his word and fulfill his promises to us. He is our restorer, deliverer, healer, and hope—He is our strength. Therefore, we can "GET UP" because He is there to pick us up.

Be encouraged today to take his hand and "GET UP!" We are not in this alone. If you do not know the Lord

Jesus Christ as your Savior, that same hand is extended to you. Reach out and take it. Ask him to forgive you for your sins and to come live in your heart. What you gain, far outweighs, what you are going to lose. So, "GET UP!" You have been down way too long.

Meditations

"That was the true light, which lighteth every man who comes into the world."

-John 1:9

The True Light

THERE ARE MANY LIGHTS in this dark world, but there is only one true light—Christ Jesus. As a child of God, we can all look back over our lives at the moments when the "true light" was there guiding us, as we maneuvered through the darkness. At times, God seems far away as the darkness blankets us. However, the truth is, He is never far at all. He is with us, always.

When we stumble—He is there to catch us; when we make a mess—He is there to clean it up, when we fall—He picks us up, when we have a financial or basic need—He provides, when sickness comes—He is our healer, when division tries to invade our relationships—He raises up a standard against the enemy, sustains us and brings unity, when our enemies come against us—He is our defense, when the storms come and our faith is being put to the test—He holds us up on the water, so that we do not sink, when we fail—He loves us and extends his compassion to us, when we are sad—He brings us joy, when we feel lonely—He is by our side whispering *"I will never leave you nor forsake you."* When anxiety tries to move in—He takes our thoughts captive and brings then into obedience with him. He gives us peace and teaches us to rest; when we lose a loved one to death—He is our comfort, when we have no one to turn to, nowhere to go, and need an answer to circumstances out of our control—He points us to His word, He gives us wisdom and makes a way out. When we pray until exhaustion sets in and we cannot find the words to go on—He sends someone to pray with us and for us. When life happens and our world is spinning out of control—He is a beam of light that will never dim or burn out. He is all that we need as we travel through the dark paths of life—His the "True Light."

Meditations

> *"My son, hear the instruction of your father, and forsake not the law of your mother: For they shall be an ornament of grace unto your head, and chains about your neck."*
>
> -Proverbs 1:8-9

Parenting Gods Way

DURING THE TIME IN which I grew up, children were taught to respect and obey their parents. Unfortunately, as time has passed, society has come to a place where such obedience and respect is obsolete. Gods word, more specifically, the book of Proverbs in Chapter one, teaches that we should conform to a relationship that is faithful to God and man.

Parents are to obey Gods word, submit to Gods ways and in return, their children are to submit to them. Parents who are guided by Gods word in a proper way, have a complete understanding of how to lead their children. As a result, when Satan, cleverly places before them the temptations of this world, they will not give in, and become bound by lustful desires.

When parents fail to lead their children according to Gods word, they are sending their children into a world of corruption, filled with temptations, they will not be equipped to stand against. They are, in essence—setting them up for failure. Their child is more likely to fall into a lifestyle of sin, which will lead to destruction.

Gods word tell us the wages of sin is death—Spiritual death. Parents be encouraged today, to walk in relationship with God. Let your daily life be a reflection of God inside of you, it may seem as though they are not interested, but at the end of the day, your children are taking it all in, and what they learn from you, is what they will ultimately exhibit to the world they live in. Parenting is the most difficult job you will ever have. Are they going to make mistakes and fail? Yes! But, with Christ as their foundation, they will also get back up and become functioning members of society.

Meditations

_____

_____

_____

_____

_____

_____

_____

_____

_____

_____

_____

_____

_____

_____

_____

_____

_____

_____

_____

_____

_____

"Take therefore no thought for tomorrow: for tomorrow shall take thought for the things of itself. Sufficient unto the day is the evil thereof."
                                        -Matthew 6:34

If Tomorrow Doesn't Come, What Did You Do Today?

ON THIS JOURNEY CALLED life, we tend to get caught up in the worries of tomorrow. We often focus on what is going to be, what could be, and what is next for our future, more so, than getting through the one day standing before us. What if tomorrow does not come? What did you do today?

We have choices, and our choices determine our outcome. We can praise, pray, and trust God to provide for us today or we can sit, worrying about finances, health, family, and friends, wondering what will be tomorrow. In the flesh, we think on things like, what we are going to eat for dinner and what we are going to wear, for some, it may be the out of town business trip scheduled or if you are a parent, how you are going to get your child to their next practice or game.

We pull out our trusty calendars and plan, writing things down to help organize our busy schedules, but what if tomorrow does not come? What did you do today? Did you help someone in need? Did you laugh and make the best of a bad situation? Did you take the time to give an encouraging word to someone? Or were you to focused on tomorrow and what is about to surface in your own life?

The things in life that do not matter—matter to us, and the things in life that should matter to us—do not. I, myself, am guilty of this. There comes a time, when we need to sit back, get alone with God, forget about tomorrow, and simply trust him to provide and bring us through today.

We get caught up in the craziness of this world, most people, spend more time going from point A to point B, than anything else. Life comes at us hard, time is passing by, and within a second our entire life can be turned upside down.

We never know when the moment will come that we exhale our last breath, it could be today, if it is, tomorrow does not matter. The only thing that matters is that we are in right standing with God. Are you saved? Do you now the Lord Jesus Christ as your Savior? If not, make today your day, step into a relationship with him. Do not put off until tomorrow, what you can do now. Step into a new life, cast your cares upon him and do not worry about tomorrow, it may not come, and if it doesn't, what did you do today?

Meditations

_____

_____

_____

_____

_____

_____

_____

_____

_____

_____

_____

_____

_____

_____

_____

_____

_____

_____

_____

_____

_____

_____

_____

"He said to me, "Son of man, can these bones live?" And I answered, "O Lord God, you know."
-Ezekiel 37:3

Spiritual Coma

HAVE YOU EVER BEEN in a place of Spiritual dryness? You go to pray, and the words will not come, you try reading the word or worshipping and find yourself, staring into space, thinking about your circumstances, rather than spending time with God. I have experienced this a few times during my Christian walk and I always ask, why?

At times it can be because we have yielded to a particular sin in our life, but more often, I believe, we get too busy. We may skip a day of prayer and worshipping God, as well as reading the word, because we just did not have time. I have always heard when you are too busy for God—then you are just too busy. In my case, I can honestly say, it was neither of those things, and God revealed to me, that He simply wanted me quiet, listening, and anticipating, what He would do next in my life.

Thankfully, God always meets us where we are. A Spiritual dry place for me seldom last longer than two or three days. I am sure we have all encountered this at one time or another, but what about a Spiritual coma? I would have to say this is much different. Spiritual coma is a term I have coined to relate to someone who is backslidden, meaning, you have stopped praying, praising, going to church, reading the word, and are slowly slipping back into your old ways, prior to getting saved. You, my friend, are in trouble.

If this describes you, I want to encourage you, by letting you now, God is waiting for you to come back to him. The only thing you need to do is, first, ask him for forgiveness, next, start thanking him for forgiving you, begin to worship him and make time for him, putting him first in your life. Come back to your first love, drink of the living water, and everything that is dry or comatose in your life will be restored, as Spiritual death gives way to life found only in Christ Jesus.

Meditations

"Martha, the sister of him who was dead, said unto Him, Lord, by this time he stinks: For he has been dead four days."

-John 11:39

Understanding Why

IN JOHN CHAPTER ELEVEN, we read about the death of Lazarus. During the time Lazarus was sick, Mary and Martha waited for Jesus to come, knowing he could heal Lazarus and keep him from dying. However, Jesus did not appear until four days after Lazarus had died, leaving Martha, Lazarus' sister asking why? Although, Jesus seemed to be too late, He was right on time and performed an even greater miracle than healing—calling Lazarus forth from the grave.

There are times in our lives when we go through a trial that leaves us desperate and devastated. We pray, believing God to move in our circumstances, and all we get is silence in return, followed by a long wait. The enemy comes along in the waiting, and oh, so subtly, whispers in our ear, that what we are believing for, is not going to happen.

Abraham and Sarah were promised a son, it was years before Isaac would be born. I am sure during their time of waiting they came to a place of not understanding why it was taking so long. At one point, they even became frustrated, taking matters into their own hands and the result was Ishmael. This is what we should never do. We should never get ahead of God or lag behind, but in all things, we must believe that at just the right moment, God will come through.

As we wait on God, we must also seek him for what he is trying to show us. Oftentimes, when we go through a trial, God is pruning and teaching us life lessons that we need to learn. In order, for us to learn and grow closer in our relationship with him, He removes the bad fruit to enable the good fruit to grow. It is a painful but rewarding process.

The sanctifying of flesh always leaves us asking, why, as we go through, but once Jesus shows up, the why questions get answered, as the miracle springs forth, the new and improved you is ready to receive the miracle, clarity comes and suddenly we understand why. Why we went through, why it took so long and why the timing of God is called, perfect. Embrace the trial you are in, let God take the reign, transform you and understand that all the answers to your whys, are on the way.

Meditations

_____

_____

_____

_____

_____

_____

_____

_____

_____

_____

_____

_____

_____

_____

_____

_____

_____

_____

_____

_____

_____

_____

_____

_____

"For everyone who asks received; and he who seeks finds; and to him who knocks it shall be opened."
-Matthew 7:8

Waiting with Patience

WAITING AND PATIENCE GO hand in hand with one another. We must maintain patience to master the process of waiting. When I take my granddaughter to meet her mother in the afternoons, we sometimes have a short wait. During our wait she will ask me several times, "where is my mommy?" She is expecting, anticipating, and looking for the arrival of her mother. After some time passes and her mother has not come, she occupies herself with a book or toy. She stops asking, which lessens her expectation and anticipation, causing her to stop looking for her mother and focus on the activity in her hand. Likewise, when we pray and are waiting for our Heavenly Father to answer, we grow impatient when the answers do not come immediately.

After a period of expecting, anticipating, and looking for the answers to manifest, we at times, stop asking. We resort to our own efforts, which takes us out of the perfect will of God. Gods word tells to seek and keep seeking, knock and keep knocking, do not quit.

If what you are praying, is the will of God for your life, He is going to answer. However, it will be in His perfect timing and not your estimated time frame. Be encouraged today to not give up on God. When you least expect it, He will come through! Lord, help us to not fall behind you or get ahead of you, but rather, walk hand in hand with you allowing you to be the patience in our waiting. Amen.

Meditations

_____

_____

_____

_____

_____

_____

_____

_____

_____

_____

_____

_____

_____

_____

_____

_____

_____

_____

_____

_____

_____

_____

_____

"Lo, I am with you always, even unto the end of the world."

-Matthew 28:20

Never Alone

LIFE HAS A WAY of taking us down a road that is engraved with many unknowns. There are events in life that can leave us stressed, grieving, and left to pick up the pieces. A part of life is dying. When we lose someone, we love, to the grip of death, navigating the grief process can be overwhelming and how we endure it, is determined primarily by our coping skills, personality, and relationship with God.

Losing a friend or loved one to death is only one cause, that leaves us experiencing feelings of loneliness. Other factors include, losing a job, pet, health, retirement, and divorce. Each of these life altering events can send us into a whirlwind of loneliness.

Feeling lonely is often accompanied by crying with the memories of the loss, depression, isolation, and inadequate or total loss of appetite. As heartbreaking as the affects of loneliness are, it is not a place we have to camp out and stay. The remedy for loneliness is the same as with every obstacle we face in life, His name is Jesus. God is our comfort.

As we spend time in prayer, we can feel His presence, as the Holy Spirit comes to meet with us. Reading his word brings consolation that fills the void of loss. Singing praises to Him, brings about joy unspeakable, and peace that surpasses all understanding, leaving no room for emptiness.

God promises to never leave us nor forsake us. He said that He would be with us, even unto the end of the world. When our time comes to transition from this life to the next, one thing we can be assured of, Jesus will be there, waiting. Whatever your loss, or cause of loneliness, put a smile on your face, and know, you are never alone. Jesus is with you, every step of the way.

Meditations

_____

_____

_____

_____

_____

_____

_____

_____

_____

_____

_____

_____

_____

_____

_____

_____

_____

_____

_____

_____

_____

"But if you forgive not men their trespasses, neither will your Father forgive your trespasses."

-Matthew 6:15

Forgiving the Unforgivable

UNFORGIVENESS IS A WILLFUL choice that we make not to forgive someone who has wronged us. The unforgiving person is selfish because their focus is on the wrong committed against them, as well as that of the perpetrator, verses being on God. Unforgiveness places a person in the position of seeking revenge, and not trusting God to deal with the perpetrator in His way.

Gods word, which is truth, tells us that vengeance is His—He will repay. The unforgiving person tends to think that by seeking revenge, they are somehow, punishing their perpetrator, when really, what they are doing, is punishing themselves. Unforgiveness only festers and plants deep within the persons heart, a spirit of bitterness, resentment, and anger, that will take root, intertwine, and choke the life out of the one who chooses not to forgive.

Unforgiveness is disobedience to God, and therefore, is a sin. Ultimately, unforgiveness will lead to other sins, such as, hatred, malice, wrath, and even murder. As a result, if the unforgiving person is a Christian, they will begin to separate from God, and if they continue in the sin, they will lose their salvation. Unforgiveness keeps the person dwelling on the past, it steals their peace and joy.

The unforgiving individual becomes like a prisoner, bound in a prison cell, and while they are living a miserable life in bondage, the perpetrator is going about their life as if nothing has happened. When my family learned that my Aunts husband had murdered her and abused her for years, we were astounded, infuriated, and in disbelief. My family felt so many different emotions, it was heart-wrenching.

We dealt with the issue of unforgiveness. However, for me personally, it was what began to turn me back to God, and God helped me to forgive my Uncle and move forward. Although, it took Gods help, I still had to make a conscious decision to forgive my Uncle and to ask for Gods help.

In spite of my feelings, I acted in Faith and trusted God to change my heart. When we forgive the person who wronged us, we turn them over to God and let Him handle them in His way. By doing that, we disarm the perpetrator and rid he or she of their ability to hold us captive through the horrific sin of unforgiveness. In addition, we have the satisfaction of knowing that when we go to God for forgiveness, He will forgive our sins.

If you need to forgive someone, why not extend to them the same gift God gave to you—the gift of forgiveness. Afterall, you were, at one time, the unforgiveable, but God forgave you.

Meditations

_____

_____

_____

_____

_____

_____

_____

_____

_____

_____

_____

_____

_____

_____

_____

_____

_____

_____

_____

_____

_____

_____

> "Come now, and let us reason together, says the
> Lord: though your sins be as scarlet, they shall be
> as white as snow."
>
> -Isaiah 1:8

Transforming Power of God

DURING THE WINTER, THE flowers cease to bloom, the grass loses its beautiful green color as it converts over to brown, the trees have shed their leaves and stand bare. All the life and colorfulness of spring and summer dissipate. However, when a fresh snow falls, it blankets the flowers, grass, and trees transforming them into something beautiful. Likewise, when a lost sinner comes to Christ he or she is Spiritually dead, but the moment they surrender their life to Jesus a transformation takes place and that which was dead, cursed by the bondage of sin, takes on a look of beauty.

The red blood of Jesus does for man, what the white snow of winter does for the flowers, grass, and trees—it transforms. It takes what was once dead and makes it beautiful. The snow will fade away as it melts and the flowers, grass, and trees will return to their original state, but with Jesus the conversion that takes place in mans heart is permanent, it will not melt away like the snow—Jesus, comes to stay!

If you do not know Jesus, as your Savior, once again I plead with you to invite Him into your heart. Trade your darkness for light and be supernaturally transformed. It will be the best decision you ever make and one that will never bring you regret.

Meditations

_____

_____

_____

_____

_____

_____

_____

_____

_____

_____

_____

_____

_____

_____

_____

_____

_____

_____

_____

_____

_____

_____

_____

> "A new commandment I give unto you, that you love one another; as I have loved you, that you also love one another."
>
> -John 13:34

Loving the Unlovable

THROUGHOUT THE BIBLE THERE are many accounts of God giving commands to the people. One of those commands Jesus gave before He was crucified, and it applies to us today. That command was to love one another in such a way that we reveal to the world, Christianity, in the form of relationship and not just another religion that leaves us at odds with others, but rather, teaches us to express love, not only to other Christians, but to everyone we come in contact with, including our enemies, those who despitefully use us, do not like us, and mistreat us—the unlovable.

How do we love the unlovable? First, we must receive Jesus Christ into our hearts and come into relationship with Him. We receive His love, then we are equipped to extend that same ardent affection to the people around us. Possessing an agape love (God kind of love) is the greatest love we can obtain as human beings, but it only comes through our faith being placed in Jesus and the grace of God being provided to us.

In return, we have what is needed to display love to everyone that crosses our path—including the unlovable. Jesus demands that we not only love our enemies, but that we pray for them, ask blessings upon them, and show them respect. If is our human nature to lash out at our enemies or anyone who mistreats us. It is difficult to love the unlovable. I have experienced this on a personal level, just as I am sure you have.

I had someone in my life, who did me wrong. After I forgave them, treated them with kindness, did things for them, they continued to hurt me emotionally, and violate my trust. I prayed for God to release me from the situation, but God kept telling me to "wait on Him" "rest" and "trust Him." In the waiting, God was teaching me how to love them, the way He does.

The reality is, God loved us when we were yet sinners, so much, that He gave His only begotten son, who died for us on a cruel, rugged cross. The love of Christ in us is what is needed to win the lost to Christ. The lost are living in the same broken world as Christians. Our behavior, and conveying Gods love, is exactly what is needed to gain the attention of those around us.

When they see joy and peace radiating from us, as we live without fear, while trapped in a world flooded with despair, they will begin to wonder—what makes us different. Therefore, it is crucial that we show love through our actions and deeds. Let the world observe the God love in us and little by little change will come as unbelievers get saved, and backsliders reconcile with God. God's love rendered to others will without fail, cause the unlovable to become lovable.

Meditations

_____

_____

_____

_____

_____

_____

_____

_____

_____

_____

_____

_____

_____

_____

_____

_____

_____

_____

_____

_____

_____

_____

_____

_____

"So, Moses brought Israel from the red sea, and they went out into the wilderness of Shur; and they went three days in the wilderness and found no water. And when they came to Marah, they could not drink of the waters of Marah, for they were bitter; therefore, the name of it was called Marah. And the people murmured against Moses, saying, what shall we drink? And he cried unto the Lord; and the Lord showed him a tree, which when he had cast into the waters, the waters were made sweet."

-Exodus 15:22-25

Obedience, Faith, and Victory

THE LORD SHOWED MOSES a tree, which was a type of the Cross. When Moses grabbed the tree and put it into the bitter waters of Marah, they were made sweet.

It was out of obedience to what the Lord was telling Moses to do and by Faith that Moses grabbed the tree and cast it into the water. First came the problem, then came obedience which followed an expression of Faith and then came the victory. If Moses had just looked at the tree and not grabbed it, the water would not have been made sweet and there would have been no victory. Likewise, when we have a problem God wants us to by Faith, be obedient to the leading of the Holy Spirit in our circumstances and grab the tree, so we to, can experience victory in our lives.

Oftentimes we are more like the children of Israel and we forget where God has brought us from and resort to murmuring and complaining followed by asking God why?

As you face trials and tribulation, do you grab the tree and hold on, wait on God, follow His lead? Or are you more like the children of Israel, quick to murmur, complain and try to figure it all out on your own? Be encouraged today to wait on God for the answers you are seeking and when He tells you to grab the tree, be obedient and by Faith grab it, put the Cross in the center of your problem and watch God work and the Victory unfold.

Meditations

_____

_____

_____

_____

_____

_____

_____

_____

_____

_____

_____

_____

_____

_____

_____

_____

_____

_____

_____

_____

_____

_____

_____

_____

"For all the promises of God in him are yea, and in him Amen, unto the glory of God by us."
                                    -II Corinthians 1:20

Promise in the Storm

THERE WILL COME A time in the believer's life, after making a specific promise, God will set them aside and carry them through a time of preparation. Gods promise to every believer is Yes and Amen, however, that does not mean the believer is immediately ready for or going to receive the promise. Oftentimes, preparation is deemed necessary by God.

Preparation is a process that includes pruning away some dead branches, allowing many tests, followed by waiting, and of course, the attacks of the enemy. The enemy's job is to block the blessing and try to deter the believer—to keep the promise from coming to fruition. Everyone has a comfort zone and moving out of that comfort zone into something new is scary.

If the enemy is successful, fear of the unknown will keep the believer in a stationary position, paralyzed, so that moving forward is not an option. At times, the enemy will take the believer in a direction that was never intended by God. In addition, the enemy will send distractions to turn the believer's attention away from the promise, and on to something irrelevant, thereby, showing the believer a way to obtain the promise that is not God's way or a part of God's plan, such was the case, with Abraham and

Sarah. The preparation process is slow and there will be opposition, storms, and as stated, a long wait.

I have been going through the preparation process for more than seven years now, and I can tell you, I have experienced every single detail mentioned. It is important to learn the lesson that God is teaching the first time, so that you do not have to continuously take the test, Let the dead branches fall and keep your focus on the promise.

Be encouraged child of God, knowing that as you go through the storm, the promise maker is in the storm with you, and His promise to you is waiting on the other side. Wait on His perfect timing and before you know it, you will come out victorious, and in possession of the promise He tailored just for you.

Meditations

_____

_____

_____

_____

_____

_____

_____

_____

_____

_____

_____

_____

_____

_____

_____

_____

_____

_____

_____

_____

_____

_____

_____

"And the Lord said unto Satan, have you considered my servant Job, that there is none like him in the Earth, a perfect and upright man, one who fears God, and eschews evil?"

-Job 1:8

Faith Unleashed

A S IT WAS WITH Job, so has it been with every Christian at some point in their walk with God—we have all been put to the test. Fortunately, for us, the tests we endure are not to the degree Job walked through. Job's faith was tested greatly, but he never wavered. While there are many lessons to be learned from Jobs experience, I believe the main lesson is, to never give up.

Job maintained his faith in God, he never gave up on life or God. No matter how hopeless your circumstance might seem, in Christ, we are victorious. There are going to be times in life, when we go through a test that requires us to stand and fight, a time when friends and family give up and think we are crazy to keep believing for something that is seemingly impossible.

Job's own wife told him to curse God and die, his friends questioned him, asking what actions he committed that would cause him such great suffering. Job was a faithful servant of God—a man of great faith. Never has a man been tested like Job and withstood the horror he went though, but Jobs faith remained, he did not curse God, he knew God would bring him out and when the test was over for

Job, God not only brough him out, but rewarded him with double what he lost.

Job unleased his faith, taking it to another level. God is waiting to do the same for us in our time of testing. His word tells us in the book of Hebrews that *"He is the same yesterday, today, and forever."* What He did for Job, He will do for us. When test come our way, no matter the test we should always ask God what He wants us to learn.

God has a redemptive plan, no matter what we lose in the process, we must not despair, instead we must unleash great faith, wait for God to deliver us, and bring us into a new dimension of his goodness. Be encouraged today to hold on to God's hand of security, unleash great faith, and trust Him to bring you out of the execrable time you are in, as only He can do.

Meditations

*"Praise you the Lord. Praise God in His sanctuary:
Praise Him in the firmament of His power."*
-Psalm 150:1

Erupt in Praise

AS CHILDREN OF GOD, there, is one thing we can be assured of, Satan has a strategic attack planned against us—a plan to break our faith. There are many ways in which he comes at us, but perhaps the most effective is—within our mind. What we think on, whether positive or negative, has a direct impact on our heart.

Satan will engage us in battle by bringing up our past sins and failures. Oftentimes, we are the ones who furnish him with the ammunition to attack us, by means of, the words we speak, what we watch on television, what we listen to on the radio, and even the company we keep.

There are people in our lives whether it be family or friends, who cannot wait for the opportunity to bring up our past, reminding us of who we were, prior to our salvation experience—yes, Satan uses other people, to successfully catapult an attack. Another way we allow him access, is by sitting and doing nothing—our mind is idle and fair game. It is at these times, we find ourselves aimlessly wandering around in our thoughts, until we have conjured up a scenario that leaves us in a state of fear. I have known people to do this until they literally, had a full-blown anxiety attack. So, how do we stop Satan in his tracks? How do we overpower him and send him packing? Erupt in praise! Open your mouth, begin to give God glory for all that He has brought you through, for His blessings in your life and for who He is!

Meditate on His word and remember His promises, that are Yes and Amen. Philippians 4:8 says, *"Finally brethren, whatsoever things are true, whatsoever things are honest, whatsoever things are just, whatsoever things are pure, whatsoever things are lovely, whatsoever things are of good report; If there by any virtue and if there by any praise, think on these things."*

Our God is worthy of all praise, all glory, and all honor. Be encouraged today to give Him the praise due to Him, let His peace reign in your mind, and Satan will have no alternative, but to flee in defeat.

Meditations

_____

_____

_____

_____

_____

_____

_____

_____

_____

_____

_____

_____

_____

_____

_____

_____

_____

_____

_____

_____

_____

"And lest I should be exalted above measure through the abundance of the Revelations, there was given to me a thorn in the flesh."

-II Corinthians 12:7

Thorn in Your Side

THE APOSTLE PAUL IN this passage of scripture and throughout was dealing with a specific issue that was causing him great problems. The word does not tell us what Paul's thorn was but alludes to it being extremely difficult to the point, it seemed as though, Satan was trying to take him out.

Paul prayed three times for God to deliver him from the infirmity, but God simply said, *"my grace is sufficient."* As a Christian we are never told that trouble will not come our way, as a matter of fact, it is the exact opposite. We are told to expect trouble and given instruction for what to do when circumstances in our life seem to be spiraling out of control. We endure, and go through, with God allowing certain things to happen as an impediment to keep us crying out to Him.

We often seek God, asking Him over and over to move in our circumstances, to answer our prayers and set us free from the thorn that seems be to be choking the life out of us. God in His wisdom knows best. At times we question God, asking Him why? Sometimes we wonder if God has heard our prayers or if He is just ignoring us, and then there are those occasions we cry out in desperation, and God responds with *"my grace is sufficient child."*

What we must understand is that God is keeping us humbled before Him. God is more concerned about our Spirit man than our flesh, and so, He is going to allow whatever it takes to keep us before Him, putting Him first, and seeking His will. If His answer continues to be a flat no, then we must trust Him, knowing that what He has purposed for our life, far outweighs and is exceedingly, abundantly, above anything we could ever ask or think.

Be encouraged today to accept Gods no, to your thorn being removed and understand—that His grace truly is sufficient.

Meditations

"And the Lord said, I have surely seen the affliction of my people which are in Egypt and have heard their cry by reason of their taskmasters; for I know their sorrows."

-Exodus 3:7

Deliverance

THE CHILDREN OF ISRAEL faced many afflictions. As God's children we also face afflictions. Every trial that comes our way as a child of God is either caused or allowed by Him for a purpose. There are many reasons for why God allows trials to come upon us. For instance, when things are going well for us, we do not pray the way we do when we are in the wilderness. God wants to hear from us constantly and at times he wants us quiet so we can hear from him.

God desires a relationship with us and like all relationships it requires talking and listening. Another reason God allows affliction is to test our faith. God wants to teach us dependence on Him, He wants to show us his provision as we go through, so by teaching us dependence and showing us how He will provide, our faith is built. At times, God allows affliction in our lives to prepare us for the call He has on our life. God wants to move us from our comfort zone; remove things and/or people from our life that may be hindering what He is trying to accomplish through us. He breaks us down, so He can build us back up, to what He wants us to be.

Finally, God allows affliction to see how we will

respond. He allows things to get as bad as they can at times, to show us our weakness. What is in us will ultimately come out of us and while God knows what is on the inside of us, we do not always know. He allows the affliction to intensify and when it does, we see things like envy, jealousy, bitterness, hate, resentment, selfishness and unforgiveness come to the surface. Once we recognize the "junk" that is not of God, then we can turn to God for deliverance and so He shows us His delivering power.

What is afflicting you today? More important, what is God trying to show you through the affliction?

Meditations

_____

_____

_____

_____

_____

_____

_____

_____

_____

_____

_____

_____

_____

_____

_____

_____

_____

_____

_____

_____

_____

_____

_____

_____

"Stand fast therefore in the liberty where with Christ has made us free and be not entangled again with the yoke of bondage."

-Galatians 5:1

Freedom from the Powers of Darkness

WHEN A MAN OR woman is arrested they are captured and become a captive, they are handcuffed, shackled and the officer holds the key to unlock the handcuffs and shackles, however, if he or she is on their way to serving a prison sentence, although, the handcuffs and shackles are unlocked and removed, they are still held captive as they are put into a prison cell. The key that unlocked the handcuffs and shackles are replaced with another key that unlocks and locks the prison cell door. They remain a captive. Likewise, when a person is in bondage to sin, they are in a spiritual prison with Satan holding the key that only locks the door.

They are a captive to the powers of darkness, with no key to unlock the door. There is only one way out and that way is to cry out to God in brokenness, and surrender. He will be faithful to hear, and He has made a way out through the blood of His son Jesus. Jesus paid the price to free us from the powers of sin and darkness.

Jesus, name above all names and freedom from sin. At the mention of His name freedom reigns; call upon His name and be free today in Jesus name.

Meditations

"You are of God, little children, and have overcome them: because greater is He who is in you, than he who is in the world."

-I John 4:4

God's Power is Greater

AS A CHILD OF God, we all go through hard times and walk through the valley of trouble. We all have enemies and unfortunately, our enemies are often those close to us, our friends, family, and neighbors. Whatever the trouble and whomever the enemy is in your life, know that there is one greater living on the inside of you, walking with you and fighting the battle for you.

When you grow weak God will revive you. When the wrath of your enemies comes against you, God will stretch forth His hand against them. His power is greater than the wrath of your enemies and the powers of darkness. Stay grounded in your faith, focused on God, and look away from the circumstances that try to hinder you. God has everything under control.

Meditations

"When Jesus came into the coasts of Caesarea Philippi, He asked his disciples, saying, whom do men say that I the son of man am?"

-Matthew 16:13

Who is Jesus Christ?

JESUS IN A MEETING with His disciples asked them *"Whom do men say that I am?"* They responded by saying, *"some say that you are John the Baptist, some Elijah, and others Jeremiah or one of the other prophets."* Jesus then asked them, *"Whom do you say that I am?"* The disciples did not respond, suggesting that they agreed with what men were saying and that Jesus was merely just another prophet. Simon Peter, however, answered Him saying *"you are the son of the living God."* Jesus replied, *"Simon for flesh and blood have not revealed it unto you, but my father who is in Heaven."* Peter's response to this question was one of Faith and an illustration of what it means to have a true relationship with God, therefore being led by the Holy Spirit.

If you had walked with Jesus and watched Him perform miracle after miracle and He asked you, *"Whom do you say that I am?"* Would your response have been one of Faith like Peter or one of unbelief like the other disciples? Who is Jesus Christ? He is the son of the living God, He is the source of all blessings, He is more than a man, He is the tried foundation of the Church, and He is a redeemer for all of humanity. Who is Jesus Christ? He is all that we need.

Meditations

"When you pass through the water, I will be with you; and through the rivers, they shall not overflow you: when you walk through the fire, you shall not be burned; neither shall the flame kindle you."

-Isaiah 43:2

No Problem is Too Big for God

THROUGHOUT ISRAEL'S HISTORY THIS verse has proven to be truth. This scripture is a prophecy that not only applies to Israel but also to Christians. As we go through this life, we are going to have problems. The key word in this scripture is *"through."*

God promises to bring us *through* the waters, *through* the rivers and He says when we walk *through* the fire. God is telling us, that as we face the problems of this life, He is all that we need to make it through.

When we step into the water (when we go into a problem) He will be with us. When we go through the rivers (the problem begins to worsen) He is our guide and when we walk through the fire (the problem gets as bad as it can, with no end in sight) the flame will not kindle upon us, because He is with us!

No matter what you are going through today, be encouraged, knowing that our Heavenly Father is with you, carrying you as you step into the water, go through the river, and trample through the fire. No problem is too big for our God!

Meditations

_____

_____

_____

_____

_____

_____

_____

_____

_____

_____

_____

_____

_____

_____

_____

_____

_____

_____

_____

_____

_____

_____

"And He said, So is the Kingdom of God, as if a man should cast seed into the ground; and should sleep, and rise night and day, and the seed should spring and grow up, he knows not how. For the earth brings forth fruit of herself; first the blade, then the ear, after that the full corn in the ear. But when the fruit is brought forth, immediately he puts in the sickle, because the harvest is come."

-Mark 4:26-29

Growing in Christ

THE PARABLE OF THE seed deals with the responsibility of believers to spread the Gospel. When the word is sown properly then the outcome will be effective. When a farmer plants a crop, first, the ground must be broken, prepared for the seed, after which comes the planting of the seed.

For the seed to grow it must go through a process. The seed will require water, fertilizer, and the light of the sun during the growth process. Once that seed is a plant, at times weeds will sprout up around it and try to stop the success of full growth. The farmer sprays chemical to kill the weeds and then the plant can finish growing to its full potential thereby producing the harvest. The seed, now a plant full of fruit, cotton, beans or whatever it bears can be harvested to go out into the world and serve its purpose. Likewise, as Christians, we must also be prepared for what God has called us to do. At times God allows events in our life to break us and free us from self, so He plants us in a position of stillness to give us one on one time with Him.

During this time God fills us with more of His Spirit, His word and He brings us into a deeper prayer life.

As we are growing in Christ, often the enemy will attack and try to stop what God is doing. It is important to remember during this time of attack that God has given us the weapons of prayer and His word. Get them out and stay in the fight! After God is finished with us, we find that we have grown Spiritually, and are now ready to do what God has for us to do. We are ready to experience victory and work the harvest. Stay in the fight! The VICTORY is worth it!

Meditations

"That you put off concerning the former conversation the old man, which is corrupt according to the deceitful lusts; and be renewed in the spirit of your mind; and that you put on the new man, which after God is created in righteousness and true holiness."

-Ephesians 4:22-24

The Sin Nature

THE APOSTLE PAUL IN this part of the epistle to the Ephesians is addressing the lifestyle that as believers we are to exhibit. Paul is explaining to the Ephesians how their former lifestyle, the way they lived before coming to Christ, should be different from the way they conduct themselves after coming to Christ—there should be a change.

The moment we are saved the sin nature is broken. Sin no longer has dominion over us. Before we were saved and living in the world, the sin nature dominated us. We did whatever we wanted, whenever we wanted, however we wanted and did not give thought to the wrong being committed or the lasting effect it would have on us.

Once we get saved, we are baptized into Christ, crucified with Him, and raised up in Him. We are a new creation in Christ Jesus, the old man, has passed away. Therefore, we do not talk the same, walk the same or look the same. There is or should be a lasting change in us that only comes from accepting Christ into our hearts.

Meditations

"Humble yourselves therefore under the mighty hand of God, that He may exalt you in due time: casting all your care upon Him; for He careth for you."

-I Peter 5:6-7

Let Your Light Shine

PETER IS WRITING THIS epistle to a group of Christians who are suffering great persecution. He is encouraging them to keep their faith, while at the same time warning them about false teachers and dealing with the commands concerning their conduct.

As Christians, how we live our lives in front of others is critical. When others see us and how we react to different situations, they should see us being a witness for Jesus—an example of who He is. Jesus, although facing death on the Cross, kept His faith in believing His Father would come through for Him. Likewise, we should humble ourselves, believing God to come through for us in every situation we face, no matter how overwhelming it may seem, it is not too hard for God.

Let your light shine that others may see Christ in you and in all things, cast your cares upon Him who cares for you.

Meditations

"Trouble and anguish have taken hold on me: yet your commandments are my delights."
-Psalm119:143

Feeling Discouraged

A S WE GO THROUGH life, we will face trouble. At times, the problems we endure will be more difficult than at other times. Life is full of ups and downs, heartache, and pain. Regardless of the magnitude of the problem, we should never forget that our help comes from the Lord.

He is always there for us to lean on and one of the ways we do that is by staying in His word. His word is our sword, our strength, our encouragement, and it holds the answer to all of life's challenges, no matter how big or small.

Whatever the problem, do not let it discourage you and turn you away from God's word, but rather let the problem carry you to God's word and dig deeper into His word as you seek out the answers you are desperate for. Meditate on His word, letting it sink deep down inside of you and although the problem may remain, the anguish will begin to fade as the peace of God consumes you and the comforter comforts you.

Be encouraged today in whatever you are facing or may be facing by the end of the day, to get into God's word and allow Him to guide you by His Spirit through the word, His word is truth and it is life, so let it lead you in the way that you should go. The answers will come and sooner than later, this too shall pass.

Meditations

_____

_____

_____

_____

_____

_____

_____

_____

_____

_____

_____

_____

_____

_____

_____

_____

_____

_____

_____

_____

_____

_____

"And he shewed me Joshua the high priest standing before the angel of the Lord, and Satan standing at his right hand to resist him. And the Lord said unto Satan, The Lord rebuke thee, O Satan; even the Lord that hath chosen Jerusalem rebuke thee: is not this the brand plucked out of the fire?"

-Zechariah 3:1-2

Salvation

THE LORD SHOWED ZECHARIAH that the true adversary to Israel was not the Samaritans or other heathen nations around them; their true adversary was Satan. The same is true for us. Our true adversary is Satan. However, as we can see in reading this scripture The Lord our God is with us, He has not left us, nor has He forsaken us. Second, we see in this passage that God is more powerful than Satan; Third, we see that God is in control, always has been, is today and always will be; Fourth, we see that God has chosen us, He didn't have to choose us, but He did, because He loves us; and fifth, we see that we are like a brand plucked out of the fire. This is what the Lord told Satan and to Israel to make them aware of what He had done for them.

This also applies to us, we to, are like a brand plucked out of the fire. Satan's plan for us was Hell's fire which is what the fire in this passage is referring to. Satan's plan of destruction for us was destroyed when we accepted the Lord Jesus Christ as our Lord and Savior. When we accepted Christ, we became the brand plucked out of the fire!

Thank God today that He has spared you from an eternal Hell and if you have not accepted God as your Savior, I pray today be the day of Salvation for you. Glory be to God!

Meditations

"And said, If thou will diligently hearken to the voice of the Lord thy God, and will do that which is right in his sight, and will give ear to his commandments, and keep all his statues, I will put none of these diseases upon you, which I have brought upon the Egyptians: for I am the Lord that health thee."

-Exodus 15:26

Healing

WHEN JESUS DIED FOR us on Calvary's Cross, He not only died for our sins but for our healing. Many people believe that healing is only for the physical body, but that is far from the truth. Jesus died so that everything that is broken in our life could be restored, not just our physical bodies.

When we came to Christ, we were instantly baptized into Him, crucified with Him, buried with Him, and raised to the newness of life. This means that we no longer live for the world, are self-serving or overcome by Satan. Getting saved is a game changer. We go from Satan having control over our lives, to Satan having to ask God's permission to come near us.

When he does gain God's permission, we are promised by God that He will not allow the test to be more than we can bear.

Sometimes the test may include sickness, but God is our healer. He has the final say. If you are sick in your body today, in a spiritual dry place, having problems in your family, marriage or facing a financial difficulty, remember Jesus died for you to be healed in EVERY area of your life. Stay focused on Him and His healing power.

Meditations

"Behold, I will make you a new sharp threshing instrument having teeth: you shall thresh the mountains, and beat them small, and shall make the hills of chaff."

-Isaiah 41:15

God Never Leaves Us

GOD PROMISED ISRAEL THAT He would not only sustain her but strengthen her to subdue her enemies. When people talk about us, raise up against us, and unjustly take advantage of us, God will give us the strength to stand against them.

As a child of God, we are not to let people intentionally take advantage of us or abuse us on any level. However, at the same time, when opposition comes, there is a way that we are to deal with the actions of other people, and it is not through retaliation. We are to show love to those who cause us pain and pray for them. If someone says something to you or about you that is hurtful or untrue, take it to the Lord and ask Him to deal with them. Do not speak harshly to that person or talk about them behind their back, that makes you their equal verses who God says you should be in Him.

I want to encourage you today to put a smile on your face and the next time that person crosses your path that has said or done something wrong to you or about you, to pay them a compliment, do not ignore them, shake their hand and speak to them first. Let the love of Christ shine through you and watch how God will turn the circumstance around working it all out for your good and Him to get the glory.

Meditations

_____

_____

_____

_____

_____

_____

_____

_____

_____

_____

_____

_____

_____

_____

_____

_____

_____

_____

_____

_____

_____

_____

_____

"Turn again, and tell Hezekiah the captain of my people, Thus says the Lord, the God of David your father, I have heard your prayer, I have seen your tears: behold, I will heal you, on the third day you shall go up unto the House of the Lord."

-II Kings 20: 5

God Will Wipe Every Tear

HEZEKIAH HAD BEGUN HIS reign with the greatest spiritual reforms ever, as well as the blessings of God which would turn his head, causing him to become prideful. He would later turn his face away from all the riches, glory, and grandeur of Judah and Jerusalem, as he saw himself undone, helpless and totally dependent on the mercy of God. With a broken heart Hezekiah would cry out to God and the Lord responded by saying *"I have heard your prayer, I have seen your tears, behold, I will heal you."*

God is no respecter of persons. Whether we are going through the loss of a loved one, a divorce, or the pain that others have a way of inflicting on us through their words and actions, one thing remains and that is Gods undying love for us. God cares for us and He sees every tear we cry.

He sees our hurt and has promised to wipe the tears, from our eyes. God is not just the healer of our physical body but also the healer of our broken hearts and emotions. Be encouraged today, knowing that the same words God spoke to Hezekiah, are for us today. Whatever the hurt, whatever the pain, God promises to hear our prayers, wipe away our tears and heal us.

Meditations

_____

_____

_____

_____

_____

_____

_____

_____

_____

_____

_____

_____

_____

_____

_____

_____

_____

_____

_____

_____

_____

_____

_____

_____

"Then He called His twelve disciples together and gave them power and authority over all devils, and to cure diseases."

-Luke 1:9

Authority in Christ

W E ARE SPIRIT BEINGS and we are constantly living in a spiritual warfare. Everything that comes against us that is not good or of God is Evil and there is a spirit behind it, including sickness. However, just like the disciples, we have been giving authority through Jesus Christ and His blood shed at Calvary's Cross, we have been given authority over the powers of darkness, as well as, the authority to lay hands on people and see them healed.

Have you ever gone through a season where the enemy attacked you from every angle? Those days when the enemy is putting thoughts in your head nonstop or causing you to worry about things that are never going to happen. We can take authority over the enemy and rebuke him in the name of Jesus. The next time the enemy is coming at you with everything he has, raise up against him and remind him that you do not live by bread alone but by every word that proceeds out of the mouth of God. Remind him who you belong to, stand against him, taking authority over him and watch how fast he will flee.

Be encouraged today knowing that you are not just starting another day, but you are starting your day with authority given to you by God through His son Jesus Christ. Go out today and conquer all that awaits you. You have got this, in Jesus name!

Meditations

_____

_____

_____

_____

_____

_____

_____

_____

_____

_____

_____

_____

_____

_____

_____

_____

_____

_____

_____

_____

_____

_____

_____

_____

> *"And as he journeyed, he came near Damascus and suddenly there shined around about him a light from Heaven, and he fell to the earth, and heard a voice saying unto him, Saul, Saul, why do you persecute me? And he said, Who are you, Lord?"*
> -Acts 9:3-5

Spend More Time with God

IN THIS SCRIPTURE WE find Saul on his way to Damascus as he branched out to other cities to persecute the church. On his way to Damascus the appearance of Christ in His Glory came before Saul and the power of God knocked him down. The encounter Saul had with God led to a transformation in him that was so great, God would change his name to Paul.

As Paul came to Christ, he realized the error in the direction for which he was headed, and he immediately made the decision to leave behind his old way of living and grasp the new plan God had for his life. Like Paul, we need to learn to let go of the things that were important to us before we accepted Christ. We need to lay down those things in our life that are taking our time away from God. This includes relationships that take too much of our time, causing us not to spend adequate time with God.

Letting go of the things and people that mean so much to us is not easy, but it is imperative that we do it. There is no relationship as important as our relationship with God. I have had to step back and let go of people in my own life. Now, I am not speaking of disowning them, but rather, cutting way back on the time you spend hanging around and communicating with them, so that you may spend more time with God.

Be encouraged today, to let go of everything in your life that is taking your time away from God. Get alone with God, in his word, and experience ALL that God has for you as He produces a new life for you to walk in. Lay down the old and pick up the new. Magnify God while setting aside what you desire. The benefits will be well worth it.

Meditations

Even so the tongue is a little member and boast great things. Behold, how great a matter a little fire kindles!

-James 3:5

The Words We Speak

THIS SCRIPTURE TELLS US that the tongue is a small member of our body, yet it has a powerful influence and is responsible for tremendous things, good and bad alike. James in this scripture is portraying the image of a forest fire starting with only one small spark.

With our tongue, we can create bad, tear down, cause destruction, bring harm to ourselves and others. On the flip side of this, the tongue also has the ability, to lift people up, encourage them, and bless them. It is often said that the physical pain we can cause a person is not as horrendous as the emotional pain we can cause them with our words. We should always be mindful of the words we speak, especially to others.

Be encouraged today to speak kind words to the people you come in contact with. Compliment them, encourage them, and bless them with your words. Speak to others the way you would have them speak to you and know that by doing so, you are pleasing the Lord Jesus Christ.

Meditations

_____

_____

_____

_____

_____

_____

_____

_____

_____

_____

_____

_____

_____

_____

_____

_____

_____

_____

_____

_____

_____

_____

_____

_____

"And they come unto Him, bringing one sick of the palsy, which was borne of four. And when they could not come nigh unto Him for the press, they uncovered the roof where He was: and when they had broken it up, they let down the bed wherein the sick of the palsy lay. When Jesus saw their faith, He said unto the sick of the palsy, Son, thy sins be forgiven thee."

-Mark 2:3-5

Press On

I N THE MIDST, OF the storms of life, have you ever wanted to just give up and quit? Have the circumstances ever been so overwhelming and looked so impossible that the only way out seemed to be to give up? I am sure as Christians we have all felt this way at one time or the other. In this scripture Jesus had just returned to Capernaum after weeks of ministering around the area of Galilee.

Arriving at the home of Peter, one of His soon-to-be disciples, noise of His return spread throughout the city, resulting in hundreds of people descending to Peter's home, filling it to capacity. In the crowd was a man who had been paralyzed for many years, lying on a cot. This man was unable to move and do for himself and as a result, he was dependent on others for everything he needed. He was not only afflicted in his physical body but Spiritually he was without God.

Depending on those helping him to move him from place to place, after he, as well as, the men carrying him, heard that Jesus was in the city, the men did all they could to get their paralyzed friend to Jesus so he could receive his miracle, believe and get saved. These men stopped at nothing to get their friend to Jesus and when they couldn't get through the crowd and the press, they managed to get him to the top of the house, remove the roof and lower him down.

The men faced an impossible situation and they could have given up, but they did not. They were determined to get their friend to Jesus, and they did. Be encouraged today not to give up. No matter what problems you are facing or how impossible your circumstances may be, stay focused on Jesus and what He can do to solve them, let your determination keep you pressing on in your walk with God and stay in the fight, determined to make it to the end!

Meditations

_____

_____

_____

_____

_____

_____

_____

_____

_____

_____

_____

_____

_____

_____

_____

_____

_____

_____

_____

_____

_____

_____

_____

PRAYER FOR SALVATION

*"Dear God in Heaven, I come to you today as a lost sinner."
"I am asking you that you save my soul and cleanse me from
all sin." "I realize in my heart my need of salvation, which
can only come through Jesus Christ." "I am accepting Christ
into my heart and what He did on the Cross in order to
purchase my redemption." "In obedience to your word, I
confess with my mouth the Lord Jesus, and believe in my
heart that God has raised Him from the dead." "You have
said in your word that whosoever calls on the name of the
Lord will be saved." "I have called upon your name as you
have said, and I believe that right now, I am saved."*

RESOURCES

For additional information about Domestic Violence and Child Maltreatment:

The American Bar Association
www.abanet.org/domviol/home.html

The Family Violence Prevention Fund
www.fvpf.org

The National Coalition Against Domestic Violence
www.ncadv.org

The Office of Justice Programs
www.oip.usdoi.gov/bis

The National Council on Juvenile and Family Court Judges
www.ncjfcj.unr.edu

U.S. Department of Justice: Bureau of Justice Statistics
www.oip.usdoj.gov/bis

Office of Juvenile Justice and Delinquency Prevention
www.ojidp.usdoi.gov

The Administration of Child Welfare
www.dhhs.gov/programs

NC Council for Women and Domestic Violence Commission
www.doa.state.nc.us/cfw/cfw.html

National Resource Center on Domestic Violence
1-800- 537-2238

The National Domestic Violence Hotline
1-800-799-SAFE (7233)

ABOUT THE AUTHOR

A CURRENT RESIDENT OF GATES County, North Carolina, Connie Smithson also worked in the Rural County for many years as a CPS Investigator/ Social Worker and Domestic Violence advocate. She graduated from College of the Albemarle with an Associates of Arts Degree, as well as Elizabeth City State University, with a Bachelor of Science degree in Criminal Justice. After completing her Bachelor of Science degree, Connie went on to obtain her Master's degree in Criminal Justice at Kaplan University. Today, Connie has dedicated her life to serving God wherever He leads. Recently, God led Connie to share her testimony surrounding her family's experience with Domestic Violence and Ministry and to make churches aware of the cries either not being heard or being ignored by leadership in the church. It is Connie's hope that this book will not only educate those who have a role in leadership in the church, but also victims of Domestic Violence, as well as, those who have direct contact with violence in the home, such as Law Enforcement, and Social Workers.

BIBLIOGRAPHY

The Expositor's Study Bible (KJV)

N.C. Department of Health and Human Services
State DHHS Manuals
http://info.dhhs.state.nc.us/olm/manuals/default.aspx

N.C. Division of Social Services
www.dhhs.state.nc.us
About Child Abuse and Neglect
www.ncdhhs.gov/dss/cps/about.htm

North Carolina General Assembly
https://www.ncleg.gov

English DJ, Widom CS, Brandford C. Childhood victimization and delinquency, adult criminality, and violent criminal behavior. 2002. {September 16th 2013}. (A replication and extension, final report (document no. 192291). https://www.ncjrs.gov

Hart, B. National Coalition Against Domestic Violence, 1988. Pg. 25

Walker, E. Lenore, The Battered Woman (pp.16-25)

Printed in the United States
by Baker & Taylor Publisher Services